THE URANTIA BOOK WORKBOOKS

URANTIA®

URANTIA FOUNDATION
533 WEST DIVERSEY PARKWAY
CHICAGO, ILLINOIS 60614
U.S.A.

URANTIA®

THE URANTIA BOOK WORKBOOKS

VOLUME VII

Terminology

This series of workbooks originally was published in the 1950s and 1960s to assist those early students who wanted to pursue an in-depth study of *The Urantia Book*. The workbook creators recognized that the materials were imperfect and were far from being definitive works on these subjects. Current students may be able to make more exhaustive analyses due to advances in knowledge and computerization of the text that are available today. Nevertheless, we recognize the enormous effort that went into this attempt to enhance understanding of *The Urantia Book* by some of its earliest students. We think these materials will be of interest to many and are therefore republishing them for their historic and educational value.

FIRST PRINTING 2003

THE URANTIA BOOK WORKBOOKS
VOLUME VII
TERMINOLOGY

The Urantia Book Workbooks

ISBN:
0-942430-93-X

PUBLISHED BY **URANTIA FOUNDATION**

Original Publisher since 1955

533 Diversey Parkway
Chicago, Illinois 60614 U.S.A.
Telephone: +1 (773) 525-3319
Fax: +1 (773) 525-7739
Website: http://www.urantia.org
E-mail: urantia@urantia.org

URANTIA Foundation has Representatives in Argentina, Belgium, Brazil, Bulgaria, Colombia, Ecuador, Estonia, Greece, Indonesia, Korea, Lithuania, México, Norway, Perú, Senegal, Spain, Uruguay, and Venezuela. If you require information on study groups, where you can obtain *The URANTIA Book*, or a Representative's telephone number, please contact the office nearest you or the head office in Chicago, Illinois.

International Offices:

Head Office

533 West Diversey Parkway
Chicago, Illinois 60614 U.S.A.
Tel.: +(773) 525-3319
Fax: +(773) 525-7739
Website: www.urantia.org
E-mail: urantia@urantia.org

Canada—English

PO Box 92006
West Vancouver, BC Canada V7V 4X4
Tel: +(604) 926-5836
Fax: +(604) 926-5899
E-mail: urantia@telus.net

Finland / Estonia / Sweden

PL 18,
15101 Lahti Finland
Tel. / Fax: +(358) 3 777 8191
E-mail: urantia-saatio@urantia.fi

Great Britain / Ireland

Tel. / Fax: +(44) 1491 641-922
E-Mail: urantia@easynet.co.uk

Australia / New Zealand / Asia

Tel. / Fax: +(61) 2 9970-6200
E-mail: urantia@urantia.org.au

Canada—French

C. P. 233
Cap-Santé (Québec) Canada G0A 1L0
Tel.: +(418) 285-3333
Fax: +(418) 285-0226
E-mail: fondation@urantia-quebec.org

St. Petersburg, Russia

Tel. / Fax: +(7) 812-580-3018
E-mail: vitgen@peterlink.ru

Other books available from URANTIA Foundation:

The URANTIA Book	hard cover			ISBN 0-911560-02-5
The URANTIA Book	leather collector ($7^5/8$" x $5^3/4$")			ISBN 0-911560-75-0
The URANTIA Book	small hard cover ($8^7/16$" x $5^1/2$")			ISBN 0-911560-07-6
The URANTIA Book	paperback		($8^7/16$" x $5^1/2$")	ISBN 0-911560-51-3
The URANTIA Book	gift-box leather ($8^7/16$" x $5^1/2$")			ISBN 0-911560-08-4
The URANTIA Book	softcover		($8^7/16$" x $5^1/2$")	ISBN 0-911560-50-5
Le Livre d'URANTIA	hard cover	French		ISBN 0-911560-05-X
Le Livre d'URANTIA	soft cover	French		ISBN 0-911560-53-X
El libro de URANTIA	paperback	Spanish	($8^7/16$" x $5^1/2$")	ISBN 1-883395-02-X
El libro de URANTIA	hard cover	Spanish	($8^7/16$" x $5^1/2$")	ISBN 1-883395-03-8
URANTIA-kirja	hard cover	Finnish		ISBN 0-911560-03-3
URANTIA-kirja	soft cover	Finnish		ISBN 0-911560-52-1
The URANTIA Book Concordance	English Index			ISBN 0-911560-00-9
The URANTIA Book	Audio	English		ISBN 0-911560-30-0
The URANTIA Book	CD ROM	English, Finnish, French		ISBN 0-911560-63-7

The URANTIA Book Workbooks

Forward and Part I	Paperback	English		ISBN 0-942430-99-9
Science	Paperback	English		ISBN 0-942430-98-0
Topical and Doctrinal Study	Paperback	English		ISBN 0-942430-97-2
Jesus	Paperback	English		ISBN 0-942430-96-4
Theology	Paperback	English		ISBN 0-942430-95-6
Bible Study	Paperback	English		ISBN 0-942430-94-8
Terminology	Paperback	English		ISBN 0-942430-93-X
Worship and Wisdom	Paperback	English		ISBN 0-942430-92-1

Dutch, Korean, Portuguese, and Russian translations also available from Urantia Foundation.

THE TERMINOLOGY OF
THE URANTIA BOOK

TERMINOLOGY OF
THE URANTIA BOOK

TABLE OF CONTENTS

QUICK REFERENCE DICTIONARY

for readers of The Urantia Book

PREFACE

While translating and editing *The Urantia Book* into Russian, we kept encountering words and phrases hard to understand. Time and again, we kept thinking: I wish there were a quick way to grasp the main meaning behind these strange-looking words! And if someone could come up with brief references on historical figures and geographic places…

We believe that every reader will share this sentiment.

Not that the world lacks explanations and references, but these are usually behind the hard covers of thick encyclopedias, dictionaries, and other reference sources. And having to look up a reference in a thick-as-a-brick folio slows down the reading and detracts attention.

So we went through the text again, this time compiling a reference for each entry that we found worth explaining. Our main goal was to make our product user-friendly. In our view, this means, first of all, economy of words. Our next criterion was the exactness of meaning. To achieve this goal, and to minimize the danger of interpretation, we used explanations found within *The Urantia Book* itself whenever possible.

Sometimes we were not sure whether an entry should be added to the list. What is self-evident to some, requires explanation to others. Perhaps a comprehensive reference source is as unlikely as a uniform understanding of the book.

We address this compilation primarily to readers of *The Urantia Book*. We understand that a scholar of the book would need in-depth references sources, and that this *Quick Reference Dictionary* would never satisfy the demands implied in a serious translation effort. But we hope that readers will find this brief compilation helpful and transparent.

Michael Hanian, compiler

Andrei Reznikov, editor

A

Aaron, 1. In Old Testament, founder and head of the Jewish priesthood.
2. Stone mason made whole by Jesus.

Abaddon, chief of the staff of Caligastia.

Abandonters, creation of the unrevealed agents of the Ancients of Days and the seven Reflective Spirits; residential citizens of Uversa.

Abbot, superior of a monastery for men.

Abel, first son of Adam and Eve to be born in the second garden.

Abila, one of the Decapolis cities east of Jordan.

Abimelech, son of Gideon, judge and hero-liberator of Israel.

Abiram, first-born son of an [unknown] Palestine king.

Abner, leader and head of the Engedi colony, the chief of John the Baptist's apostles.

Abram, *see* Abraham.

Abraham, 1. First of the Hebrew patriarchs.
2. Member of Sanhedrin who espoused the teachings of Jesus.

Absalom, third and favorite son of David, king of Israel and Judah.

Absoluta, Uversa appellation for space potency.

Absolute Mind, mind of The Infinite Spirit.

Absolute reality, three existential persons of Deity, the Isle of Paradise, and the three Absolutes.

Absolute Trinity, second experiential Trinity of God the Supreme, God the Ultimate, and the Consummator of Universe Destiny.

Absolutum, unique substance of Paradise.

Absonite reality, reality which is relative with respect to both time and eternity.

Achaia, historic region of Greece on the N coast of the Peloponnese peninsular.

Acropolis, natural historic center of Athens, rising some 500 feet above sea level.

Acts of the Apostles, fifth book of the New Testament.

Actium, peninsular on the W coast of Greece near the site of naval battle where Octavian [future emperor Augustus] defeated Mark Antony [Roman general under Julius Caesar].

Actual, realities existing in fullness of expression; that which was and is.

Actuary, one who calculates insurance and annuity premiums, reserves, and dividends.

Adam^1, 1. First Material Son of Satania.
2. Material Son of Urantia, number 14,311 of the senior corps of Material Sons and Daughters on Jerusem.
3. Generic name of Material Sons of Satania.

Adam^2, ancient town in Perea.

Adamites, *see* **violet race.**

Adamson, first-born son of Adam and Eve.

Adamsonites, descendants of Adamson.

Aden, "strange preacher" who became a believer in Jesus through the testimony of Amos [*see* **Amos, 3**].

Adirondack Mountains, mountains in NE New York state, U.S.A.

Adjutant Mind Spirits, Supreme Spirits, children of the Universe Mother Spirit; personal ministry of a local universe Mother Spirit on the teachable level of material mind.

Administrative Assistants, first group of the administrator seraphim; immediate assistants of a System Sovereign.

Administrator Seraphim, fourth seraphic order; organized into 7 groups, perform administrative functions in local systems.

Adonai [Hebrew *My Lord*], one of the Hebrew replacements for Yahweh.

Adonia, ancient commercial metropolis in the Central Asia.

Advanced Adjusters, Thought Adjusters who have served with Spirit-fused creatures.

Aegean, of or relating to the arm of the Mediterranean Sea east of Greece.

Agaman, widow of Damascus, member of the women's evangelistic corps.

Agni, fire-god of the Hindus.

Agondonters, ascenders from isolated worlds.

Ahab, [9th century BC] seventh king of the N kingdom of Israel [reigned c. 874-c. 853 BC].

Ahura-Mazda [Avestan *Wise God*], deity of goodness and light in Zoroastrianism.

Ai, ancient Canaanite town destroyed by the Israelites under Joshua.

Akkad, ancient region in what is now central Iraq, the N [or NW] division of ancient Babylonian civilization.

Alabaster, fine-textured usually white and translucent gypsum.

Alexander, 1. Alexander the Great [BC 356-323] king of Macedonia and conqueror of Greek city-states and of the Persian empire.

    2. Alexandrian banker, brother of Philo.

    3. Son of Simon from Cyrene.

Alexandria, ancient and modern city on the Mediterranean Sea at the estern edge of the Nile Delta; capital of Egypt between 332 BC to AD 642.

Alexandrian, 1. Having to do with Alexandria.

    2. Built during lifetime of Alexander the Great.

Allah, [Arabic *God*] the one and only God in the religion of Islam.

Almighty Supreme, evolving God of time and space; nonpersonal expression of the thriune Paradise Deity; the power unification of the grand universe Creators.

Alpha and Omega, in Christianity, the first and last letters of the Greek alphabet, used to designate the comprehensiveness of God, implying that God includes all that can be.

Alpheus twins, *see* **James Alpheus** *and* **Judas Alpheus.**

Alps, mountain system of south-central Europe.

Alvoring, local universe in Orvonton.

Amadon, modified human associate of Van.

Amadonites, descendants of the 144 andonites, whose leader was Amadon.

Amatha, mother-in-law of Simon Peter.

Amathus, ancient town in Perea.

Amaziah, Judean king of the 8th century BC.

Amdon, Chaldean herder, the first human to meet Machiventa Melchizedek.

Amenemope, ancient Egyptian prophet and teacher, author of the Book of Wisdom.

Amenhotep III, [also *Nebmaatre*] king of Egypt of the 18th dynasty.

American Federal Union, *here* the United States of America.

Amida Buddha, [from *Buddha Amitabha*, "the Buddha of Infinite Light"] name of Buddha in Pure Land Buddhism.

Ammonites[1], ancient Semitic people whose principal city was Rabbath Ammon, in Palestine.

Ammonites[2], extinct cephalopods with flat spiral shells.

Amorites, ancient Semitic people who dominated the history of Mesopotamia, Syria, and Palestine from about 2000 to about 1600 BC.

Amos,   1.   Hebrew prophet in the 8th century BC.
      2.   Youngest brother of Jesus.
      3.   Kheresa lunatic.
      4.   Friend of John Mark.

Amosad, Andite leader about 15,000 BC; regenerated Sethite priesthood.

Anatolia, peninsula in W Asia.

Anaxagoras, [500-428 BC] Greek philosopher of nature.

Anaxand, Greek youth who met Jesus in Caesarea.

Ancients of Days, Supreme Trinity Personalities; the rulers of the superuniverses.

Andes Mountains, great mountain system of S America.

Andites, mixed race of the Nodites, Adamites, and Sangik tribes.

Andon, ["the first Fatherlike creature to exhibit human perfection hunger"] first man of Urantia.

Andonites, descendants of Andon and Fonta.

Andovontia, tertiary Universe Circuit Supervisor stationed in Nebadon.

Andrew, first chosen apostle of Jesus, chairman of the apostolic corps of the kingdom.

Andromeda, far-distant nebula outside the inhabited part of Orvonton.

Andronover, nebular, which served as the basis for creation of the local universe of Nebadon.

Ang, member of the corporeal staff of Prince Caligastia; head of the council on food and material welfare.

Angamon, leader of the Stoics whom Jesus taught in Rome.

Angelic World, third transition culture world.

Anglo-Saxons, Germanic peoples who originally migrated from northern Germany to England.

Angona, physical system which triggered the formation of the solar system.

Animism, 1.   Attribution of conscious life to objects in and phenomena of nature or to inanimate objects.
      2. Belief in the existence of spirits separable from bodies.

Anna, poetess who wrote a hymn of the redemption of the baby Jesus.

Annan, Nodite member of the Urantia reception committee.

Annas, high priest emeritus; father-in-law of Caiaphas and relative of Salome.

Annon, one of the ancestors of Mary, mother of Jesus.

Anova, oldest inhabited world of Satania.

Ansie, one of the ancestors of Mary, mother of Jesus.

Antares, stellar cloud; largest star in Nebadon.

Anthropomorphism, interpretation of what is not human or personal in terms of human or personal characteristics, humanization.

Antigravity, local influence of the Infinite Spirit which neutralizes gravity.

Antioch,   1.   Ancient capital of Syria.

2.   [Antioch Pisidian] ancient town in Phrygia.

Antioch cult, *here* Pauline Christianity.

Antipatris, ancient town on the Plain of Sharon, in central Palestine.

Antonia, fortress of, Roman citadel in ancient Jerusalem named after the younger daughter of Mark Antony.

Anu, one of the ancestors of Mary, mother of Jesus.

Apennines, [Apennine Range] arc of mountains forming the backbone of peninsular Italy.

Aphrodite, Greek goddess of love and beauty.

Apocalyptic, forecasting the ultimate destiny of the world.

Apocalyptists, new school of religious teachers which appeared in Palestine about one hundred years before Jesus, concerned with the intervention of God in history.

Apollo, Greek and Roman god of sunlight, prophecy, music, and poetry.

Appalachian Mountains, [Appalachians] great highland system of eastern N America.

Appian Way, first of the ancient Roman roads, running from Rome to Campania and S Italy.

Aquila, Roman Jew, tentmaker, one of the Cynics whom Jesus taught in Rome; later a Roman Jewish Christian.

Arabia, peninsular in SW Asia.

Arabian Sea, NW arm of the Indian Ocean.

Arabs, historically, Semitic inhabitants of the Arabian Peninsula; in a broader sense, Arabic-speaking peoples.

Aram, ancient region in N Syria.

Aramaic, Semitic language originally spoken by the ancient people of Aram, known as Aramaeans.

Arbela, ancient town in Perea.

Archangels, Universe Aids, offspring of the Creator Son and the Universe Mother Spirit; dedicated to the work of creature survival and to the furtherance of the ascending career of the mortals.

Archelais, ancient town in central Palestine.

Archelaus, *see* **Herod Archelaus.**

Archeozoic, prelife era; began 1 billion years ago, lasted 450 million years.

Associate Inspectors

Architects of Being, unrevealed order; formulate plans for construction of life.

Architects of the Master Universe, the governing corps of the Paradise Transcendentalers; exist in seven levels of the absonite.

Architectural spheres, space bodies constructed for their special purpose.

Ardnon, leader of a group of Chaldean priests who knew of Michael's impending bestowal.

Areopagus, [Greek *Ares' Hill*] earliest aristocratic council of ancient Athens.

Areopolis, ancient town in Perea.

Arimathea, ancient town in Samaria.

Aristotle [384-322 BC], ancient Greek philosopher, pupil of Plato and tutor of Alexander the Great; his works range all branches of ancient learning.

Arius, [AD 250- 336] Christian priest of Alexandria whose doctrine, according to which Christ is not truly divine but a created being, was denounced by the early church as a major heresy.

Armageddon, [probably *Hebrew Hill of Megiddo*] headquarters of the orange race; *see also* **Megiddo.**

Armenia, country in Transcaucasia.

Aroer, ancient town in Perea.

Artemis of the Ephesians, Greek goddess of wild animals, the hunt, and vegetation, and of chastity and childbirth.

Aryans, descendants of the Turkestan and Mesopotamian Andites.

Ascending Pilgrims, courtesy colony; assigned to various services in connection with their Paradise progression.

Ascendington, one of the Paradise satellites; sacred world of the Father, the "bosom of the Father, Son, and Spirit"; contains the mystery of evolution of the immortal soul in the mortal mind.

Ascension, evolutionary spiritual and mindal growth of created beings; experiential discovery-career of the realization of God.

Ashdod, town in S Palestine, on the coastal plain of ancient Philistia.

Ashtaroth, ancient town in Bashan.

Ashtoreth, Canaanite goddess of love and war, mod. of Astarte.

Ashur, city god of Ashur and national god of Assyria.

Ashurbanipal, last of the great kings of Assyria; reigned 668-627 BC.

Asia Minor, *see* **Anatolia.**

Asmonean dynasty, dynasty of ancient Judea, descendants of the Maccabee; founded by Hasmoneus.

Asoka [Ashoka], last major emperor in the Mauryan dynasty of India.

Assigned Sentinels, Higher Personalities of the Infinite Spirit, offspring of the Infinite Spirit; coordinating personalities and liaison representatives of the Seven Supreme Executives.

Assistant Teachers, fourth group of superior seraphim; helpers and associates of the teaching counselors.

Associate Inspectors, Higher Personalities of the Infinite Spirit, joint offspring of the Infinite Spirit and the Seven Master Spirits; the personal embodiment of the authority of the Supreme Executives to the local universes.

Associate Power Directors, Master Physical Controllers; administrators, inspectors, and instructors in the field of energy regulation.

Associate Registrars, Morontia Power Supervisors; morontia world recorders.

Associate Transcendental Master Force Organizers, beings of unrevealed origin; transmute energy from the primary through the secondary or gravity-energy stage.

Assuntia, local system in Nebadon.

Assyria, kingdom of N Mesopotamia, the center of a great empire of the ancient Middle East.

Astarte, goddess of the ancient Near East, chief deity of Tyre, Sidon, and Elath, worshipped in Egypt and Ugarit and among the Hittites, as well as in Canaan.

Athanasius, [AD 293-373] theologian, ecclesiastical statesman, and Egyptian national leader; chief defender of Christian orthodoxy in the 4th-century battle against Arianism.

Athens, historic city and capital of Greece.

Atman, in Hinduism, the soul or self, self-recognition.

Aton, in ancient Egyptian religion, a sun god, depicted as the solar disk emitting rays terminating in human hands.

Attis, mythical son of Cybele; worshipped in Phrygia, Asia Minor, and later throughout the Roman Empire.

Augustus, [Gaius Octavius, subsequently Gaius Julius Caesar Octavianus, still later Augustus or Caesar Augustus, 63 BC-AD 14] the first Roman emperor, following the republic.

Aurora, a luminous phenomenon that consists of streamers or arches of light appearing in the upper atmosphere of a planet's magnetic polar regions.

Autocracy, government in which one person possesses unlimited power.

Avalon, local universe in Orvonton.

Avonals, *see* **Magisterial Sons.**

Azariah, [Uzziah] son and successor of Amaziah, and king of Judah for 52 years (c. 791-739 BC).

B

Ba, concept of the soul in ancient Egypt and parts of Africa.

Baal, god worshipped in many ancient Middle Eastern communities, especially among the Canaanites.

Baal-Perazim, place where King David defeated the Philistines.

Babel, center of culture of Nodites and Andites.

Babel, tower of, monument od Nodite culture, named after Bablot, the architect and builder of the tower; unfinished tower fell of its own weight.

Bablod, *see* **Babel**.

Bablot,   1.   Descendant of Nod; architect of the tower of Babel.
    2.   *see* **Babel**.

Babylon, capital of Babylonia.

Babylonia, ancient empire in Mesopotamia.

Badonan, great-great-grandson of Andon.

Badonan tribes, superior Andonites, who settled in the NW India.

Baganda, [Ganda] people inhabiting the area N and NW of Lake Victoria in south-central Uganda.

Bagdad, [Baghdad] ancient and modern city in Mesopotamia, modern Iraq.

Balkans, [Balkan peninsula] easternmost of Europe's three great southern peninsulas.

Balm of Gilead, [balm of Mecca] myrrhlike resin from *Commiphora opobalsamum* [trees and shrubs of the incense-tree family] of Arabia.

Baluchistan, historical region in S Asia.

Banshees, female spirit in Gaelic folklore whose appearance or wailing warns a family that one of them will soon die.

Baptism, 1. Christian sacrament marked by ritual use of water and admitting the recipient to the Christian community.

 2. Non-Christian rite of using water for ritual purification.

Barabbas, agitator, robber, and murderer released by Pontius Pilate.

Barak, Naphtalite, chief commander of Deborah.

Barnabas, [Joseph the Levite] early Christian missionary.

Bartholomew, father of apostle Nathaniel.

Bartimeus, blind man healed by Jesus in Jericho.

Bashan, ancient country, located in what is now Syria.

Basques, people who live in both Spain and France in areas bordering the Bay of Biscay and encompassing the W foothills of the Pyrenees Mountains.

Batanea, area to the N of Decapolis.

Bathsheba, wife of Uriah the Hittite; later became one of the wives of King David and the mother of King Solomon; one of the ancestors of Mary, mother of Jesus.

Bautan, pupil of Gautama who imparted to his teacher the traditions of the Salem missionaries.

Bedouins, nomadic peoples of the Middle Eastern deserts, especially of Arabia, Iraq, Syria, and Jordan.

Beelzebub, leader of the disloyal midway creatures.

Beeroth, ancient town in central Palestine.

Beersheba, ancient and modern town in S Israel.

Beirut, largest city of Lebanon, lies on the Mediterranean coast.

Beit Adis, ancient village in the vicinity of which Jesus spent the forty days after his baptism.

Beit Jenn, ancient village in the foothills of Mount Hermon.

Bel, [Enlil] god of the atmosphere and a member of the triad of gods completed by Anu [An] and Ea [Enki].

Belgium, country in W Europe.

Bel-Marduk, chief god of the city of Babylon and the national god of Babylonia; was eventually called simply Bel, or Lord.

Benares, [Varanasi] town in SE Uttar Pradesh state, N India.

Bengal, historic region in the NE part of the Indian subcontinent.

Berbers

Berbers, indigenous peoples of N Africa, largely scattered in tribes across Morocco, Algeria, Tunisia, Libya, and Egypt.

Bering Strait, strait linking the Arctic Ocean with the Bering Sea and separating the continents of Asia and N America at their closest point.

Bernice, mother of Justa.

Bestowal, [of a Son of God] personalization and factualization of a Son of God on one of the evolving levels of a local universe.

Bestowal Attendants, supreme seraphim of the first group who accompany Paradise Avonals on bestowal missions.

Bethany,   1.   Ancient village on the slopes of Mount Olivet.
   2. Bethany beyond Jordan, ancient village in Perea.

Bethabara, *see* Bethany, 2.

Bethel, [Luz] ancient town in Palestine, located N of Jerusalem.

Bethesda, pool of water with natural hot spring in Jerusalem.

Bethlehem, town in Judea.

Bethlehem of Galilee, ancient town in Galilee.

Beth-Marion, Phoenician woman who dwelled at the Bethsaida camp.

Beth-Meon, ancient town in Perea.

Beth-Nimrah, ancient town in Perea.

Beth-Peor, ancient town in Perea.

Bethphage, village near Bethany.

Bethsaida, [traditionally *Hierapolis*] fishing harbor of Capernaum.

Bethsaida-Julias, ancient town to the NE of the Galilean Sea.

Beth-shean, ancient Hebrew name of Scythopolis.

Beth-zur, ancient village in Judea.

Bildad, [Shuhite] comforter of Job.

Binary star, pair of stars in orbit around their common center of gravity.

Bithynia, ancient district in NW Anatolia.

Black Forest, [Schwarzwald] mountain region in SW Germany.

Black Sea, inland sea situated at the SE extremity of Europe.

Black Hills, mountain region in W South Dakota and NE Wyoming, U.S.A.

Blue race, one of the three primary evolutionary races of Urantia.

Bon, member of the corporeal staff of Prince Caligastia; head of the board of animal domestication and utilization.

Book of the Dead, ancient Egyptian collection of mortuary texts made up of spells or magic formulas.

Book of Job, Old Testament book.

Book of Proverbs, Old Testament book of "wisdom" writing.

Book of the Law, [Sefer Torah] in Judaism, the first five books of the Old Testament.

Book of Psalms, Old Testament book composed of sacred songs, or of sacred poems.

Books of the Maccabees, four books appearing in some manuscripts of the Septuagint [the Greek version of the Old Testament].

Borneo, island SE of the Malay Peninsula in the Greater Sunda group of the Malay Archipelago.

Bosora, [Bostra] ruined town S of Damascus; served as a key Roman fortress east of the Jordan.

Brahma, in the late Vedic period of India, one of the major gods of Hinduism.

Brahman, 1.   In Indian philosophy, that which is the greatest, also characterized as infinite, truth, and knowledge and as existence, consciousness, and bliss.
2. Member of the high caste of priests.

Brahmanas, prose commentaries attached to the Vedas.

Brahman-Narayana, supreme deity usuually identified with Vishnu.

Breath Giver, Andonite deity concept in the times of Onagar.

Brenner Pass, mountain pass, one of the lowest and most important through the main chain of the Alps.

Bright and Morning Stars, Universe Aids; offspring of the Creator Son and the Creative Spirit; first-born Sons and chief administrators of local universes.

Brilliant Evening Stars, Universe Aids; unique twofold order of the local universe Sons embracing some of created dignity and others of attained service; perform different assignments, both in pairs and in groups.

British Columbia, westernmost province of Canada.

British Isles, group of islands off the W coast of Europe.

Brittany, historical province in the NW France.

Broadcasters, superior seraphim of the sixth group; dispatch records and disseminate essential information.

Bronze Age, third phase in the development of material culture among the ancient peoples of Europe, Asia, and the Middle East, following the Paleolithic and Neolithic ages.

Brown race, offspring of the early red and yellow men.

Brownie, in English and Scottish folklore, a small, industrious fairy or hobgoblin believed to inhabit houses and barns.

Buddhism, religion of E and central Asia growing out of the teaching that suffering is inherent in life and that one can be liberated from it by mental and moral self-purification.

Burma, [Myanmar] country in SE Asia.

Burnt offering, oblation through the medium of the fire, the most common means of making an offering, be it animal or vegetation, available to sacred beings.

Bushmen, group of short-statured peoples of S Africa who traditionally live by hunting and foraging.

Busiris, town in Lower Egypt.

C

Caesar, any of the Roman emperors succeeding Augustus Caesar.

Caesar Augustus, *see* **Augustus**.

Caesarea, ancient port and administrative city of Palestine, on the Mediterranean coast.

Caesarea Philippi, ancient town near the headwaters of the Jordan River.

Caiaphas, high priest of Israel.

Cain, son of Cano and Eve.

Caleb, in the Old Testament, one of the spies sent by Moses to spy out the land of Canaan.

Calebites, in the Old Testament, descendants of Caleb.

Caledonian Mountains, range of mountains situated in northwestern Europe.

Caligastia, Lanonandek Son, number 9,344 of the secondary order; former Planetary Prince of Urantia, joined the Lucifer rebellion.

Caligastia one hundred, *see* **corporeal staff**.

Caligula, [Gaius Caesar Germanicus, AD 12-41] Roman emperor from 37 to 41.

Callirrhoe, ancient town in Perea.

Calvary, *see* **Golgotha**.

Cambrian, first period of the Paleozoic era; lasted 50 million years.

Cana, town in Galilee close to Nazareth.

Canaan, area variously defined, but always centered on Palestine.

Cano, leader of a colony of friendly Nodites, who seduced Eve.

Cape Horn, headland on Isla [island] Hornos in S Chile.

Capernaum, ancient city on the NW shore of the Sea of Galilee.

Capetown, [Cape Town] legislative capital of the Republic of S Africa.

Capitolias, ancient town in Perea.

Capitolium, [Capitolium Temple] temple at Cosa, NE of Rome, conceived in the 3rd century BC and dedicated to Jupiter, Juno, and Minerva.

Cappadocia, ancient district in east-central Anatolia.

Capua, in ancient times, the chief city of the Campania region of Italy.

Carboniferous age, fifth period of the Paleozoic era; lasted 45 million years.

Caribbean Sea, suboceanic basin of the W Atlantic Ocean.

Carpathians, crescent-shaped mountain range in east-central Europe.

Carrara marble, world's finest marble from Massa-Carrara province in north-central Italy.

Carthage, ancient town traditionally founded on the N coast of Africa by the Phoenicians.

Caspian Sea, world's largest inland sea, lying E of the Caucasus Mountains.

Caspin, ancient town in Perea.

Caste,   1.   One of the hereditary social classes in Hinduism.

    2.   Division of society based on differences of wealth, inherited rank or privilege, profession, or occupation.

Castor oil, [ricinus oil] nonvolatile fatty oil obtained from the seeds of the castor bean.

Castration, deprivation of the testes or of the ovaries.

Cataclysm, momentous and violent event marked by overwhelming upheaval and demolition; catastrophe.

Catalepsy, condition of suspended animation and loss of voluntary motion in which the limbs remain in whatever position they are placed.

Catskill Mountains, segment of the Allegheny Plateau, U.S.A., and part of the Appalachian system.

Cedes, believer from Antioch who made a brief record about Jesus used by Luke.

Celestial Artisans, sevenfold courtesy colony; composite order of artists and artisans of the morontia and lower spirit realms engaged in morontia embellishment and in spiritual beautification.

Celestial Guardians, Trinitized Sons, offspring of perfected humans and of Paradise-Havona personalities; officers of the courts of the Ancients of Days.

Celestial musicians, specialized group of celestial artisans; produce celestial harmony by the manipulation of morontia and spirit energies.

Celestial Overseers, Universe Aids; inspectors of the Nebadon school technique.

Celestial Recorders, Messenger Hosts of Space, ascendant seraphim from the local universes; execute all records in duplicate, making an original spirit recording and a semimaterial counterpart.

Celsus, believer who guested Jesus and the twelve in Caesarea-Philippi.

Celta, daughter of a Roman centurion; member of the women's evangelistic corps.

Cenozoic, mammalian era; occupies the last 50 million years.

Census Directors, Higher Personalities of the Infinite Spirit, creation of the Infinite Spirit; become immediately aware of the birth of will in any part of the grand universe and register such events.

Centaur, creature fabled to be half man and half horse.

Ceylon, [Sri Lanka] island country in the Indian Ocean.

Chaldea, ancient land in S Babylonia [modern S Iraq].

Chang, Chinese merchant whom Jesus met in Corinth.

Charax, [former Antiochia] capital of Characene, ancient state in the S of Babylonia.

Chazan, [*also* hazan, hazzan, chazzan] *here* overseer of the synagogue.

Chedorlaomer, leader of the coalition of Mesopotamian kings defeated by Abraham.

Chemism, *here* chemical energy.

Chemosh, ancient West Semitic deity, revered by the Moabites as their supreme god.

Cherubim, angelic order, offspring of a Universe Mother Spirit; ministering spirits of the local universes, assistants of seraphim.

Ch'in Shih Huang Ti, [c. 259-210/209 BC] emperor of the Ch'in dynasty and creator of the first unified Chinese empire.

Chlorophyll, green photosynthetic pigment found chiefly in the chloroplasts of plants.

Chorazin, ancient town on the NW bank of the Sea of Galilee.

Christ Michael, *see* **Michael of Nebadon**.

Chronoldeks, frandalanks that register time in addition to quantitative and qualitative energy presence.

Chuza, steward of Herod Antipas.

Cicero, [Marcus Tullius Cicero, 106-43 BC] Roman statesman, lawyer, scholar, and writer.

Cincinnati Island, geological uplift in Middle Devonian period on the site of modern Cincinnati in Ohio, USA.

Circuit, *here* system of circulation of physical, mindal, or spiritual energy.

Circuit Regulators

Circuit Regulators, Morontia Power Supervisors; coordinate physical and spiritual energy and regulate its flow into the segregated channels of the morontia spheres.

Circuit Spirits, *see* **Spirits of the Circuits**.

Circuit Supervisors, *see* **Universe Circuit Supervisors**.

City of David, *see* **Bethlehem**.

City of Judah, ancient town W of Jerusalem.

Claudia Procula, wife of Pontius Pilate.

Claudius, Roman slaveholder who spent one evening with Jesus.

Claudus, downhearted young man who met Jesus on Malta; later a preacher of the Cynics, and still later a Christian missionary.

Cleavages, splitting of a crystallized substance or rock along definite planes.

Clement, [AD 150-betw. 211 and 215] Christian Apologist, missionary theologian to the Hellenistic world, and teacher of the catechetical school of Alexandria.

Cleopas, one the two brothers who met morontia Jesus.

Cloa, one of the ancestors of Mary, mother of Jesus.

Clopas, husband of Mary, one of the women, who stood at the cross of Jesus.

Coabsolute, compatible with absolute reality.

Coal age, *see* **Carboniferous age**.

College of Administration, one of local universe Melchizedek schools.

College of High Ethics, part of the Melchizedek University; highest training in the universe administration.

College of Personalized Adjusters, school for Personalized Adjusters on Divinington.

College of Spiritual Endowment, part of the Melchizedek University; highest training of the spiritual evangels of Nebadon.

College of Wisdom, school of wisdom and truth on Salvington.

Colorado River, major river of N America, rising in the Rocky Mountains.

Combined Controllers, Morontia Power Supervisors; mechanical beings; sensitive to, and functional with, physical, spiritual, and morontial energies.

Comforter, *see* **Spirit of Truth**.

Completion seraphim, Son-Spirit ministers; members of the Seraphic Corps of Completion.

Compound manipulators, celestian artisans; belong to energy manipulators; deal with functional association of the three original phases of divine energy.

Conductors of Worship, special corps of primary seraphim, directing worship and perfecting its expression on Paradise.

Confucius, [Kung-Fu-tse, 551-479 BC] Chinese philosopher and teacher.

Conjoint Actor, *see* **Infinite Spirit**.

Conjoint Creator, *see* **Infinite Spirit**.

Constantine, [Constantine the Great, AD 280-337] first Roman emperor to profess Christianity.

Constellation, structural unit of a local universe.

Constellation Fathers, [Most Highs] Vorondadek Sons, rulers of constellations.

Consummator of Universe Destiny, unrevealed order.

Corinth, ancient and modern city of the Peloponnesus, in south-central Greece.

Cornelius, Roman centurion who became a believer in Jesus through Peter's ministry.

Corporeal staff, ascending beings, rematerialized citizens of a system capital; serve as advisers and helpers of the Planetary Prince in the work of early race improvement.

Corps of Light and Life, *see* **Corps of Mortal Finaliters**.

Corps of Mortal Finaliters, Paradise corps of evolutionary creatures who have achieved perfection in everything which pertains to God's will.

Corps of Mortal Finality, *see* **Corps of Mortal Finaliters**.

Corps of Perfection, local universe corps for Spirit-fused ascenders.

Cosmic circles, *see* Psychic circles.

Cosmic force, all energies deriving from the Unqualified Absolute and (yet) unresponsive to Paradise gravity.

Cosmic mind, mind, distributed by the Seven Master Spirits in the grand universe; known in types and variants, such as the Nebadon variant of the Orvonton type of cosmic mind.

Council of Equilibrium, high commissioners of power dispatched by the Seven Master Spirits from the personnel of the Associate Master Force Organizers; direct and distribute Master Physical Controllers from the headquarters of the superuniverses.

Court Advisers, second group of the supreme seraphim; advisers and helpers attached to all orders of adjudication in the local universe.

Courtesy colonies, 7 colonies, sojourn on the architectural spheres; dedicated to science, art, education, and creature ascension.

Crab nebula, an irregular nebulae; remnant of a supernova.

Creative Agencies of the Ancients of Days, unrevealed order.

Created Corps, *see* Brilliant Evening Stars.

Creative Daughter, *see* Creative Spirit.

Creative Spirits, offspring of the Infinite Spirit; creative partners of the Creator-Sons of local universes.

Creator Sons, [Michaels] Sons of God, creators of local universes.

Creature-trinitized sons, beings trinitized by creatures.

Cretaceous, third period of the Mesozoic era; lasted over 50 million years.

Crete, island in the E Mediterranean.

Crispus, chief ruler of the synagogue in Corinth at the time of Jesus' Mediterranean tour.

Cro-Magnoids, individuals with some Cro-Magnon characteristics.

Cro-Magnons, ancient European race produced by the blending of the Andites with the blue men.

Custodians of Records, Messenger Hosts of Space, tertiary supernaphim; keepers of the formal archives of Paradise.

Cuthites, inhabitants of the ancient city-state Cuthah in Mesopotamia, N of Kish.

Cutites, unknown Asian tribes.

Cybele, [Great Mother of the Gods] ancient Oriental and Greco-Roman deity, known by a variety of local names.

Cymboyton

Cymboyton, wealthy merchant citizen of Urmia.

Cynics, ancient Greek school of philosophers who held the view that virtue is the only good and that its essence lies in self-control and independence.

Cyprus, island in the NE Mediterranean Sea.

Cyrene, ancient Greek colony in Libya.

Cyrus, [?-530 BC] founder of the Achaemenid empire, centered on Persia and comprising the Near East from the Aegean Sea to the Indus River

D

Dabaritta, ancient town in Galilee.

Dagon, [Dagan] West Semitic god of crop fertility, worshipped extensively throughout the ancient Middle East.

Dalamatia, headquarters of the Planetary Prince on Urantia.

Daligastia, secondary Lanonandek, number 319,407 of the secondary order; assistant of Caligastia.

Damascus, capital of Syria.

Dan[1], member of the corporeal staff of Prince Caligastia; head of the advisers regarding the conquest of predatory animals.

Dan[2], ancient town near the headwaters of the Jordan River close to Caesarea Philippi.

Daniel, Hebrew prophet during the times of the Babylon captivity.

Danube, river in Europe, second longest after the Volga.

Daphne, beautiful daughter of a river god who rejected every lover, including Apollo.

Dark gravity bodies, enormous dark masses, sorrounding Havona and arranged in two belts.

Dark islands of space, extinct suns or large aggregations of matter devoid of light and heat.

Daughter Spirit, *see* **Creative Spirit**.

David, second of the Israelite kings, who established a united kingdom over all Israel, with Jerusalem as its capital.

David Zebedee, brother of John and James Zebedee; head of the messenger corps of the kingdom.

Daynals, *see* **Trinity Teacher Sons**.

Dead Sea, landlocked salt lake between Israel and Jordan, the lowest body of water on Urantia.

Deborah, prophet and heroine who inspired the Israelites to a mighty victory over their Canaanite oppressors.

Decapolis, league of 10 ancient Greek cities in E Palestine.

Deccan, plateau region in S India.

Decimal planets, life-experiment worlds.

Declaration of Liberty, manifesto stating the cause of the Lucifer rebellion.

Deity, source of divinity; functions on prepersonal, personal and superpersonal levels.

Deity Absolute, [Qualified Absolute] self-qualified I AM; causational, potentially personal possibilities of total reality, the absolute of Deity potential.

Deliberative assembly, legislative or advisory council of the superuniverse.

Deliverer, 1.   Jewish Messiah.

2.   *See* **Jesus of Nazareth.**

Denarius, small silver coin of ancient Rome.

Depression, *here* area lower than the surrounding surface.

Descending Sons, orders of divine creation, dedicated to the descending ministry to the worlds and systems of time and space; include Paradise Sons of God and Local Universe Sons of God.

Designers and embellishers, specialized group of celestial artisans; masters of morontia and spiritual color, sound, emotion, odor, presence embellishment, taste, and synthesis.

Deuteronomy, fifth book of the Old Testament.

Devonian, fourth period of the Paleozoic era, the age of fishes; lasted 50 million years.

Devouress, in ancient Egyptian religion, hybrid creature, who destroyed the souls of those whose heart was heavy.

Diadem, crown, a royal headband; something that adorns like a crown.

Dilmat, Egyptian name for Dilmun.

Dilmun, town in Mesopotamia; headquarters of Nodites after the submergence of Dalamatia.

Diogenes, [414-323 BC] archetype of the Cynics.

Dion, [Dium] one of the Decapolis cities in Perea.

Dionysus, [Bacchus] in Greco-Roman religion, a nature god of fruitfulness and vegetation, especially known as a god of wine and ecstasy.

Directors of Assignment, fifth group of the supreme seraphim; high council co-ordinating the self-directed phases of seraphic service and assignment.

Directors of conduct, primary supernaphim; instruct the new members of Paradise society in the usages of the perfect conduct of the high beings.

Discerners of Spirits, secondary seconaphim; reflect the actual moral and spiritual character of any individual.

Dispensation, an era in the spiritual evolution of an inhabited world; inaugurated by advent of a divine Son of planetary service.

Dives, rich man in the parable about the rich man and the beggar.

Divine builders, specialized group of celestial artisans; plan, construct, and re-model morontia and spirit abodes.

Divine Counselors, Stationary Sons of the Trinity; the counsel of Deity to the realms of the seven superuniverses.

Divine executioners, Universal Conciliators qualified to make contact with the material beings and to execute the decisions of the commission.

Divine Minister, *see* **Creative Spirit.**

Divinington, one of the Paradise satellites; sacred world of the Father, the "bosom of the Father"; contains the secret of the bestowal and mission of Thought Adjusters.

Divinity, characteristic, unifying, and coordinating quality of Deity.

Dolomite, mineral consisting of a calcium magnesium carbonate.

Dominant, controlling genetic character or factor.

Don, river in Russia.

Dorcas, [Tabitha] believer from Joppa.

Dothan, ancient settlement in Samaria.

Double star, *see* **binary star**.

Dravidians, mixed race from the blending of the Andites with the native stock of India.

Drumlin, oval or elongated hill believed formed by the streamlined movement of glacial ice sheets across rock debris, or till.

Dualism, *here* doctrine that the world [or reality] consists of two basic, opposed, and irreducible principles that account for all that exists.

Dyaks, [Dayaks] non-Muslim indigenous peoples of S and W Borneo [modern Kalimantan].

Dyaus, Sanskrit name for the chief of the "high gods."

E

Ea, Mesopotamian god of water and a member of the triad of deities completed by Anu [Sumerian *An*] and Bel [Enlil].

Easter Island, island in the E Pacific Ocean.

Eastern Ghats, mountain range in S India.

Ebal, biblical mountain, twin of Mt. Gerizim, in central Palestine.

Eber, officer of the Sanhedrin, who became a believer in Jesus.

Ecclesiastes, Old Testament book of "wisdom" literature.

Echinoderms, radially symmetrical coelomate marine animals.

Eden, *see* **Garden of Eden**.

Edenites, inhabitants of Eden.

Edentia, headquarters of the constellation of Norlatiadek.

Edrei, ancient town in Perea.

Edomites, descendants of Edom (Essau), son of Isaac and Rebekah.

Egypt, country in NE Africa.

El, [Semitic *God*] chief deity of the West Semites.

El Elyon, [Hebrew *God Most High*] name of God revealed by Machiventa Melchizedek.

El Shaddai, [Hebrew *God, the One of the Mountains*] Egyptian concept of the God of heaven accepted by Hebrews.

Elam, ancient country in SW Iran.

Elealah, ancient town in Perea.

Eleusinian mysteries, secret religious rite of ancient Greece.

Elihu, prophet of Ur and priest of the Salem believers.

Elijah, one of the twenty-four counselors; spiritual teacher and prophet in Ephraim.

Elijah Mark, father of John Mark.

Eliphaz, [Temanite] comforter of Job.

Elisha, Israelite prophet, the pupil of Prophet Elijah, and also his successor.

Elizabeth, 1.   Mother of John the Baptist and kinswoman of Mary, mother of Jesus.
2.   Member of the women's evangelistic corps.

Ellanora, loyal leader of Panoptia mortals after the outbreak of the Lucifer rebellion.

Elman, Syrian physician who supervised the Bethsaida hospital.

Elohim, [singular *Eloah*] Sumerian-Chaldean name for the Trinity; established as three-in-one God concept in Hebrew theology during the Babylon captivity.

Emmaus, ancient town in Judea.

Enchanter, person who practices sorcery.

Endantum, world of the bestowal incarnation of Michael of Nebadon as a morontia mortal.

Endogamy, marriage within a specific group as required by custom or law.

Endor, ancient town in Galilee.

Energy manipulators, specialized group of celestial artisans; manipulate physical, mindal, and spiritual energies.

Energy Transformers, Master Physical Controllers, offspring of the Seven Supreme Power Directors and the Seven Central Supervisors; maintain universal energy balance; change the physical form of the energies of space.

Energy Transmitters, Master Physical Controllers; living superconductors for the most forms of physical energy.

En-Gannim, ancient town in Galilee.

Engedi, colony of Nazarites by the Dead Sea.

English Channel, arm of the Atlantic Ocean separating the S coast of England from the N coast of France.

Enoch, one of the twenty-four counselors; son of Cain and Remona, first of the mortals of Urantia to fuse with the Thought Adjuster during the mortal life in the flesh.

Enos, son of Seth; founder of the new order of worship.

Ensa, minor sector number 3 in the major sector of Splandon.

Enseconaphim, to become prepared for seconaphim transport.

Enseraphim, to become prepared for seraphic transport.

Enta, one of the ancestors of Mary, mother of Jesus.

Eocene, first period of the Cenozoic era; lasted 15 million years.

Ephesus, ancient Greek town in Ionian Asia Minor.

Ephraim, 1.   Hebrew tribe which gave origin to the Kingdom of Israel.
2.   Ancient town in Judea.

Epicureanism, dedication to the pursuit of happiness as the chief good.

Erech, [Uruk] ancient Mesopotamian city-state located NW of Ur [modern SE Iraq].

Error, willful rejection of truth, misconception or distortion of reality.

Esdraelon, lowland in N Israel, dividing the hilly areas of Galilee in the north and Samaria in the south.

Eskimos, native population of the Arctic and sub-Arctic regions of Greenland, Alaska, Canada, and far E Russia.

Essenes, religious sect or brotherhood that flourished in Palestine from about the 2nd century BC to the end of the 1st century AD.

Esta, wife of James, brother of Jesus.

Esther, Jewish wife of the Persian king Ahasuerus; persuaded the king to retract an order for the general annihilation of Jews throughout the empire.

Eternal Son, Original Son of God, the Second Source and Center, the absolute of spirit.

Eternals of Days, Supreme Trinity Personalities; rulers of the Havona worlds.

Ethical Sensitizers, fourth group of supervisor seraphim; foster and promote the growth of creature appreciation of the morality of interpersonal relationships.

Etruscans, ancient people of Etruria, in Italy.

Eugenics, science that deals with the improvement of hereditary qualities of a race or breed.

Euphrates, largest river in W Asia.

Evangel of Light, any celestial personality assigned to the service of any finaliter corps.

Eve,   1. First Material Daughter of Satania.
   2. Material Daughter of Urantia, number 14,311 of the senior corps of Material Sons and Daughters on Jerusem, the third physical series.
   3. Generic name of Material Daughters of Satania.

Evening Stars, *see* **Brilliant Evening Stars**.

Eventod, name of Michael as an ascendant pilgrim of mortal origin during the fifth bestowal.

Eveson, second son of Adam and Eve.

Evil, partial realization of, or maladjustment to, universe realities; partiality of creativity which tends toward disintegration and eventual destruction; measure of imperfection in universe interpretation.

Evolutionary religion, experience of primitive worship, a mind derivative.

Existential, extra- and superexperiential.

Ex officio, [*Latin*] by virtue or because of an office.

Exogamy, marriage outside of a specific group esp. as required by custom or law.

Experiential, pertaining to experience.

Extension, *here* broad meaning [*cf.* intension].

Extension-School Instructors, courtesy colony; teachers of the next higher world on the world just below.

Extensiveness, *here* broad meaning.

Ezda, orphan of Beth-zur.

Ezekiel, prophet-priest of ancient Israel.

Ezra,   1. Religious leader and reformer who reconstituted the Jewish community on the basis of the Torah.
   2. Merchant and trader of Nazareth.
   3. Jew from Syracuse who found God through Jesus.
   4. Disciple of John the Baptist.

Ezraeon, Alexandrian friend of Joseph and Mary.

F

Fad, member of the corporeal staff of Prince Caligastia; head of the faculty on dissemination and conservation of knowledge, formulated the first alphabet.

Fahrenheit, Daniel Gabriel, German physicist and maker of scientific instruments. $°F = (9/5 \times °C) + 32$.

Fair Havens, ancient port on Crete.

Faithful of Days, Supreme Trinity Personalities; Paradise representatives in the constellations.

Faith sons, status of the mortals of time and space prior to Adjuster fusion.

Fandor, passenger bird; became extinct over thirty thousand years ago.

Fanoving, local universe in Orvonton.

Fantad, one of the twenty-four counselors; spiritual leader of the green men about 350,000 years ago.

Far East, regions of Asia facing the Pacific Ocean.

Faroes, group of islands in the N Atlantic Ocean.

Far West, western areas that are, unlike Far East, not clearly defined.

Fates, in Greek and Roman mythology, three goddesses who determine the span of a person's life and his allotment of misery and suffering.

Father Melchizedek, local universe Son, offspring of Creator Son and Creative Spirit; cocreator of the cognominal order.

Feast of tabernacles, [Sukkot; Hebrew *Huts* or *Booths*] Jewish autumn festival of double thanksgiving.

Feast of dedication, (Hanukka; Hebrew *Dedication*] Jewish festival commemorating the rededication [164 BC] of the Second Temple of Jerusalem.

Finaliter, member of the Corps of the Finality.

Finaliter World, first transition culture world.

Finite reality, reality projected in space and actualized in time.

First Source and Center, *see* **Universal Father**.

Flavius,   1.   Greek Jew and proselyte, later believer in Jesus.

  2.   Host of Greek believers in Jerusalem.

Fonta, ["the first Sonlike creature to exhibit human perfection hunger"] first woman of Urantia.

Force organizers, *see* **Master Force Organizers**.

Formosa, [Portuguese *beautiful*] another name for Taiwan given by Portuguese explorers.

Fortant, secondary Lanonandek; bestowal director of Satania.

Fortune, Cretan youth who found faith through Jesus; leader of the Christians in Crete in the 1st century AD.

Fossil, remnant, impression, or trace of an organism of past geologic ages that has been preserved in the Urantia's crust.

Four and twenty councelors, present advisory-control body of Urantia located on Jerusem and directly representative of Michael and Gabriel.

Foxhall peoples, first Andonites to settle in England.

Frandalanks, Master Physical Controllers, joint creation of force organizers and power directors; living and automatic presence, pressure, and velocity gauges.

Fused Adjusters, Adjusters who have become one with the ascending creatures of the superuniverses.

Fusion Adjusters, Adjusters capable of the fusion with their wards.

G

Gabriel, Bright and Morning Star of Nebadon.

Gad, one of the tribes of Israel which settled on land east of the Jordan River.

Gadara, one of the Decapolis cities, located SE of the Sea of Galilee.

Gadda, ancient town in Perea.

Gadiah, Philistine interpreter whom Jesus met in Joppa.

Gaius, friend of Crispus whom Jesus met in Corinth; later a supporter of Paul.

Galantia, associate of Gavalia.

Galatia, ancient district in central Anatolia.

Galilee, northernmost region of ancient Palestine.

Gamala, town in Galilee.

Gamaliel, teacher and master of the Jewish Oral Law.

Ganges, river in N India.

Ganges Bay, northernmost part of Bay of Bengal of the Indian Ocean.

Ganid, Indian pupil of Jesus during the Mediterranean tour.

Garden of Eden, 1. Planetary headquarters of Adam and Eve in Asia Minor [first garden].

    2. Headquarters of Adamites in Mesopotamia [second garden].

Gath, one of the five royal cities of the Philistines; exact location unknown.

Gautama Siddhartha, Indian religious teacher, philosopher and prophet in the 6th century BC.

Gavalia, first-born Brilliant Evening Star of Nebadon.

Gaza, town in SW Palestine.

Geba, town in S Palestine.

Gehenna, *see* **Hinnom**.

Genghis Khan, [12th century AD] founder of the Mongol Empire.

Gennesaret, ancient settlement on the W cost of the Sea of Galilee.

Gentile, person who is not Jewish.

Gerar, ancient town in S Palestine.

Gerasa, one of the Decapolis cities in Perea.

Gerizim, *see* **Mount Gerizim**.

Germ plasm, germ cells and their precursors serving as the bearers of heredity and being fundamentally independent of other cells.

Geshur, ancient country SE of Bashan.

Gethsemane, garden across the Kidron Valley on the Mount of Olives.

Gibeon, ancient town in Palestine, located NW of Jerusalem.

Gibraltar, channel connecting the Mediterranean Sea with the Atlantic Ocean.

Gideon, [*also* Gedeon, Jerubbaal, Jerobaal, 11th century BC] judge and hero-liberator of Israel.

Gilboa, mountain in Samaria.

Gilead,   1.   Area of ancient Palestine east of the Jordan River. 2. Ancient town in Perea.

Gileadites, Israelite tribe of Gilead.

Gischala, [Giscala] ancient town in Galilee.

Glantonia, a local system in Nebadon.

Globular cluster, approximately spherical clusters of gravitationally associated stars.

Glorified, *here* Paradise-attained.

Gobi, desert in East Asia.

Goblins, ugly or grotesque sprite that is mischievous and sometimes evil and malicious.

Godad, hermit keeper of traditions of the Melchizedek missionaries in the days of Gautama.

God the Absolute, experientializing God of transcended superpersonal values and divinity meanings.

God the Father, First Person of Deity.

God the Son, Second Person of Deity.

God the Spirit, Third Person of Deity.

God the Sevenfold, sevenfold Deity personalization in time and space and to the seven superuniverses.

God the Supreme, evolving God of time and space; personality expression of the triune Paradise Deity; supreme Creator and supreme creature.

God the Ultimate, eventuating God of supertime and transcended space.

Golden rule, fundamental ethical principle: "Do to others as you would be done by".

Golgotha, [Aramaic *Skull*] also called Calvary [from Latin **calva** *bald head* or *skull*], skull-shaped hill in Jerusalem.

Goliath, Philistine giant slain by David.

Gonod, Indian merchant and father of Ganid.

Gophna, ancient town in central Palestine.

Gradant, standard weight on Jerusem [ten Urantia ounces].

Graduate Guides, Higher Personalities of the Infinite Spirit; directors of the high university of technical instruction and spiritual training of Havona; prepare the ascending pilgrims for admission to Paradise and the Corps of the Finality.

Grand Canyon, immense gorge cut by the Colorado River into the high plateaus of NW Arizona, U.S.A.

Grandfanda, first evolutionary mortal to complete the Paradise ascension.

Grand Lama, reincarnation of a great saint or teacher ranked by the Dalai Lama.

Grand universe, central universe together with the seven superuniverses.

Gravita, Uversa appellation for universe power.

Gravity energy, second phase of the transmutation of primordial force.

Gravity Messengers

Gravity Messengers, Supreme Spirits, modified and personalized Adjusters; messengers of the primary Corps of the Finality, able to transcend time and space.

Greater Road, *see* Mahayana.

Great Lakes, chain of lakes in east-central N America comprising Lakes Superior, Michigan, Huron, Erie, and Ontario.

Great Mother, cult originated by the descendants of Cain in Crete.

Great River, in Egyptian mythology, the river separating the world of the living from the world of the dead.

Great Spirit, single Deity in the teachings of Onamonalonton.

Greece, country occupying the southernmost extension of the Balkan Peninsula.

Greenland, world's largest island in the N Atlantic Ocean.

Greensand, sedimentary deposit that consists largely of dark greenish grains of glauconite often mingled with clay or sand.

Green race, one of the three secondary evolutionary races of Urantia; absorbed by the indigo race.

Guardians of destiny, personal seraphic guides of the children of time.

Guild, association of people with similar interests or pursuits.

Guites, ancient tribes of N Mesopotamia.

Gulf Stream, warm ocean current flowing in the N Atlantic.

H

Hades, in Greek mythology, ruler of the underworld, "the House of Hades".

Hagar, [*also* Agar] Abraham's concubine and the mother of his son Ishmael.

Haggai, prophet who helped mobilize the Jewish community for the rebuilding of the Temple.

Hallel, [Hebrew *Praise*] Jewish liturgical designation for **Psalms 113-118** ("Egyptian Hallel") as read in synagogues on festive occasions.

Hamathites, population of the ancient city-state Hamath in Assyria.

Hammurabi, sixth and best-known ruler of the 1st (Amorite) dynasty of Babylon.

Han, second great Chinese Imperial dynasty, considered the prototype for all later Chinese dynasties.

Hanavard, primary Lanonandek; high counselor of Satania.

Hannah, mother of Mary and grandmother of Jesus.

Hap, member of the corporeal staff of Prince Caligastia; head of the college of revealed religion.

Haran, ancient town in Mesopotamia.

Harmony supervisors, tertiary supernaphim; insure harmony in the work of preparing the pilgrims of time for Paradise achievements.

Harmony workers, specialized group of celestial artisans; manipulate and organize forces and energies not recognized by mortals.

Hatita, ancient town in Perea.

Havona, central and divine universe.

Havona energy, pre-existent, triune phase of energy which is characteristic of the central universe.

Havona natives, creation of the Paradise Trinity; nonreproducing, fusion-type beings who may evolve in status.

Havona Servitals, Messenger Hosts of Space, joint creation of the Seven Master Spirits and the Seven Supreme Power Directors; "midway creatures" of the central universe.

Hearts of Counsel, secondary seconaphim; reflect the superaphic intelligence co-ordinators; selectively reflective of the counsel of all beings, high or low.

Heavenly reproducers, specialized group of celestial artisans; celestial harmonists, painters, and dramatists.

Hebron, ancient and modern town south-southwest of Jerusalem.

Heidelberg race, superior tribes which spread over Europe about 900,000 years ago.

Heldua, ancient town on the Phoenician coast.

Hellene, native or inhabitant of ancient Greece.

Hellenic, of or relating to ancient Greek history, culture, or art before the Hellenistic period.

Hellenist, person living in Hellenistic times who was Greek in language, outlook, and way of life but was not Greek in ancestry; esp. a hellenized Jew.

Hellenistic,1. Relating to Greek history, culture, or art after Alexander the Great. 2. Of or relating to the Hellenists.

Henotheism, worship of one god without denying the existence of other gods.

Henselon, local universe in Orvonton.

Herbivorous, feeding on plants.

Herod Agrippa, [Agrippa I, 10 BC-AD 44] grandson of Herod the Great; king of Judaea [AD 41-44].

Herod Antipas, [21 BC-AD 39] son of Herod the Great; tetrarch of Galilee [4 BC-AD 39].

Herod Archelaus, [22 BC-AD 18] son and principal heir of Herod the Great as king of Judea, deposed by Rome because of his unpopularity with the Jews.

Herod Philip, [20 BC-AD 34] son of Herod the Great, ruled as tetrarch over the former NE quarter of the kingdom of Judaea.

Herod the Great, [Idumean, 73-4 BC] Roman-appointed king of Judaea [37-4 BC].

Herodians, party of influential Jewish supporters of the Herodian dynasty.

Herodias, wife of Herod Antipas; conspired to arrange the execution of John the Baptist.

Heshbon, ancient town in Perea.

Hestia, in Greek religion, goddess of the hearth, daughter of Cronus and Rhea, and one of the 12 Olympian deities.

Hezekiah, [late 8th and early 7th centuries BC] son of Ahaz, and the 13th successor of David as king of Judah at Jerusalem.

Hierapolis, ancient Phrygian town in SW Turkey.

Hieroglyphics, system of writing mainly in hieroglific, or pictorial, characters.

High Commissioners, Universe Aids, Spirit-fused ascendant mortals; interpret the viewpoints and portray the needs of the various human races.

High Son Assistants, trinitized offspring of perfected humans and of Paradise-Havona personalities; function as personal aids in the governments of the Ancients of Days.

Hildana, woman forced to become prostitute and saved by Jesus.

Himalayas, loftiest mountain system in the world, form the N limit of India.

Hinayana, [Sanskrit *Lesser Vehicle*] the more orthodox, conservative school of Buddhism; cf. Mahayana.

Hinduism, beliefs, practices, and socioreligious institutions of the peoples known as Hindus that have evolved from Vedism.

Hindu Kush, mountain system of Central Asia.

Hinnom, [Gehenna], valley west and south of Jerusalem where originally children were burned as sacrifices to the Ammonite god Moloch; later was made a garbage center to discourage a reintroduction of such sacrifices.

Hippos, one of the Decapolis cities east of the Jordan River.

Hiram, Phoenician king of Tyre [reigned 969-936 BC].

Hittites, ancient Indo-European people who appeared in Anatolia at the beginning of the 2nd millennium BC.

Holdant, tertiary Lanonandek; custodian of Satania.

Holocene, sixth [postglacial] period of the Cenozoic era; occupies the last 35 thousand years.

Holy Spirit, spiritual circuit of the Creative Daughter.

Honan, province in Central China.

Honen Shonin, Buddhist priest, founder of the Pure Land [Jodo] Buddhist sect of Japan.

Hood, *see* **Mount Hood**.

Horeb, *see* **Mount Sinai**.

Horus, [*also* Hor, Har] in ancient Egyptian religion, god in the form of a falcon whose eyes were the sun and the moon.

Hosea, first [8th century BC] of the canonical Twelve [Minor] Prophets.

Hudson Bay, inland sea indenting east-central Canada.

Hudson River, river within New York state, U.S.A.

Hydrogen chloride, colorless pungent poisonous gas.

Hydrosphere, aqueous envelope of a planet including bodies of water and aqueous vapor in the atmosphere.

I

I AM, expression of the transcendental concept of God.

Iceland, large island in the N Atlantic.

Ichthyosaurs, extinct marine reptiles.

Ideograph, picture or symbol used in a system of writing to represent a thing or an idea but not a particular word or phrase for it.

Idumea, [Edom], ancient land bordering ancient Israel, in what is now southwestern Jordan, between the Dead Sea and the Gulf of Aqaba.

Ikhnaton, [*also* Akhenaton, Amenhotep IV, Neferkheperure Amenhotep] king of Egypt of the 18th dynasty, who established a new monotheistic cult of Aton.

Image Aids, *see* **Reflective Image Aids**.

Imhotep, [27th century BC] vizier, sage, architect, astrologer, and chief minister to Djoser, the second king of Egypt's third dynasty.

Immanence of the Projected Incomplete, living presence of the evolving Supreme Being.

Immanuel of Salvington, Union of Days assigned to the local universe of Nebadon.

Import of Time, tertiary seconaphim; evaluate and analyze time, both past and future.

Incantation, 1.   Use of spells or verbal charms spoken or sung as a part of a ritual of magic.

2.   Written or recited formula of words designed to produce a particular effect.

Incarnation, embodiment of a deity or spirit in some earthly form.

Indigo race, one of the three secondary evolutionary races of Urantia.

Indo-China, [Indochina] peninsula in SE Asia.

Indra, chief of the Vedic gods of India; a warlike Aryan god.

Indus, river in S Asia.

Infinite Spirit, Third Source and Center; the absolute mind.

Initiation, rites, ceremonies, ordeals, or instructions with which one is made a member of a sect or society or is invested with a particular function or status.

Inspiration, divine influence or action on a person believed to qualify him or her to receive and communicate sacred revelation.

Inspired Trinity Spirits, mysterious offspring of the Paradise Trinity; possibly function as teachers of the realms by superconscious techniques.

Intelligence Corps, first group of the superior seraphim; belong to the personal staff of Gabriel.

Intension, [of a concept] essential meaning of a concept [*cf.* extension].

Intensiveness, *here* narrow meaning.

Intercession, prayer, petition, or entreaty in favor of another.

Interpreters of Cosmic Citizenship, third group of the administrator seraphim; quicken appreciation of the responsibilities of universe government.

Invertebrates, animals lacking a spinal column.

Iron, town in Galilee.

Iroquois federation, nonsurviving confederation of the Indian tribes of Mohawks, Oneidas, Onondagas, Cayugas, Senecas, and Tuscaroras.

Irrigate, supply with water by artificial means.

Isaac,   1.   Son of Abraham.

2.   Moneylender from Nazareth.

Isador, disciple of Apostle Matthew who wrote the second Gospel.

Isaiah,   1.   [The first, 8th century BC] Hebrew prophet.

2.   [The second, 6th century BC] Hebrew prophet.

Ishtar, [Akkadian] goddess of war and sexual love.

Isis, [*also* Aset, Eset] important goddess of ancient Egypt, mother and wife of Osiris.

Islam, world religion founded by the Arabian apostle, or prophet, Muhammad in the 7th century AD.

Isle of Paradise, timeless and spaceless center of master universe; dwelling place of the eternal Paradise Deities; the center of the force-energy activation of the cosmos.

Israel,   1.   Northen kingdom in Palestine between 11th and 8th centuries BC.

2.   Jewish People.

J

Jabbok, river joining the Jordan from the E.

Jacob,   1.   Hebrew patriarch, grandson of Abraham.

2.   Stone mason, neighbor and friend of Jesus in Nazareth and husband of Miriam, sister of Jesus.

3.   Jewish trader from Crete who met Jesus in Jerusalem.

4.   Leader of the younger evangelists. 5. One of David's messengers.

6.   Resident of Emmaus who talked with morontia Jesus.

Jacob's well, well in Samaria, 9 ft wide and 75 ft deep; according to the Bible, dates back to the times of Jacob [*see* **Jacob, 1**].

Jah, [Hebrew *Yah*] Semite term for God used as an alternative to speaking God's name; the first syllable of Jehovah meaning primal force or spirit word .

Jainism, religion and philosophy of India, founded in the 6th century BC.

Jairus, ruler of the synagogue in Capernaum.

James, brother of Jesus.

James Alpheus, apostle of Jesus.

James of Safed, official of Herod Antipas and father of the epileptic healed by Jesus.

James Zebedee, apostle of Jesus.

Jamnia, ancient town in Judea.

Jansad, first son of Eveson.

Japhia, ancient town in Galilee.

Jaram the Hittite, student of Melchizedek at Salem.

Java, Indonesian island.

Jebus, ancient Canaanite town.

Jehoash, father of the first king of Israel, Jeroboam.

Jehonadab, one of the leaders in the revolt against the worshippers of Baal.

Jehovah, Judeo-Christian name for God, derived from Yahweh.

Jehu, leader of the revolt, which extinguished the dynasty of Omri.

Jephthah, judge or regent of Israel who sacrificed his daughter to Yahweh in fulfill-ment of a vow setting the price of victory.

Jeramy, Greek proselyte who guested Jesus in Nicopolis.

Jeremiah, Hebrew prophet, reformer, and author of an Old Testament book that bears his name.

Jericho, town in Judea.

Jeroboam, son of Jehoash and the first king of Israel [reigned 922-901 BC].

Jerusem, headquarters of the local system of Satania.

Jesus of Nazareth, human incarnation of Michael of Nebadon during his bestowal in the likeness of creatures.

Jethro, priest of Midian of the Kenite clan, father-in-law of Moses.

Jezebel, daughter of the priest-king Ethbaal, king of the Sidonians, and wife of King Ahab.

Jezreel, ancient town in Galilee and capital of the N kingdom of Israel under King Ahab.

Joab, head of the corps of evangelists.

Joachim, father of Mary, mother of Jesus.

Joanna, member of the women's evangelistic corps.

Joash, 8th king of Judah in the 8th century BC.

Job, Old Testament book found in the third section of the biblical canon.

Jogbehah, ancient town in Perea.

Johab, bridegroom at the Cana wedding.

John Hyrcanus, high priest of Judaea [from 76 to 40 BC] and last of the Maccabean [Hasmonean] dynastic rulers.

John Mark, disciple of Jesus and author of the earliest Gospel.

John Zebedee, apostle of Jesus.

John the Baptist, forerunner of Michael's mission on Urantia.

Jonah, in the Old Testament, one of the Minor Prophets.

Joppa, [Jaffa] ancient coastal settlement in Palestine.

Jordan, river in Palestine; lowest river in the world.

Jose, renowned Nazareth rabbi in the times of Jesus.

Joseph,   1.   Father of Jesus.
> 2.   Great-grandson of Abraham.
> 3.   Brother of Jesus.
> 4.   Believer from Tyre.

Joseph of Arimathea, secret disciple of Jesus.

Joshua, leader of the Israelite tribes after the death of Moses, who conquered Canaan and distributed its lands to the tribes.

Joshua ben Joseph, Hebrew name of Jesus.

Josiah,   1.   16th king of Judah [640-609 BC] who set in motion a reformation that bears his name.
> 2.   Blind beggar healed by Jesus in Jerusalem.
> 3.   Disciple of Abner.

Jotapata, ancient town in Galilee.

Joys of Existence, secondary seconaphim; promote and upstep reactions of joy and pleasure of the realms; improve the humor taste and develop a superhumor among mortals and angels.

Judaism, monotheistic religion developed among the ancient Hebrews that holds that God's presence is experienced in human actions and history.

Judah, head of the southern Hebrew clan.

Judas Alpheus, apostle of Jesus.

Judas Iscariot, apostle of Jesus.

Judas Maccabee, hero of the Jewish wars of independence, 168-164 BC.

Jude, brother of Jesus.

Judea, S Hebrew kingdom in Palestine.

Judges, book of the Old Testament containing the history of the judges [ancient leaders of Israel].

Julias, ancient town in Perea.

Juno, in Roman religion, chief goddess and female counterpart of Jupiter.

Jupiter,   1.   Chief Roman and Italian god.

2.   Largest planet in the solar system.

Jurassic, second period of the Mesozoic era; lasted about 25 million years.

Justa, Syrian woman who guested Jesus in Sidon.

Justice Guides, second group of the administrator seraphim; prepare the statements for preliminary hearings involving mortal survival.

Justus,   1.   Merchant from Corinth with whom Jesus visited during the Mediterranean tour.

2.   One of the two candidates for the position of apostolic treasurer after the betrayal of Judas Iscariot.

K

Ka, in ancient Egypt and parts of Africa, individual's double, endowed with all the person's qualities and faults.

Kaaba, [Ka'bah] shrine located near the center of the Great Mosque in Mecca.

Kaaba stone, Black Stone of Mecca located in the E corner of the Kaaba.

Kanata, [Canatha] one of the Decapolis cities in N Palestine.

Kansu, province in NW China.

Karahta, ancient town in Galilee.

Karkar, ancient fortress in W Syria.

Karma, force generated by a person's actions held in Hinduism and Buddhism to perpetuate transmigration and to determine the nature of the person's next existence.

Karuska, Syrian woman who guested Jesus near Sidon.

Kashmir, historical area in Asia, in the upper basin of Indus.

Kateri [*also* Parbate, Khasa, or Chetri] people of mixed descent in Nepal and Himalayan India.

Katro, head of the family whith whom Machiventa Melchizedek lived for over 30 years.

Keilah, ancient Canaanite town.

Kenan, grandson of Seth; instituted the foreign missionary service of the second garden.

Kenites, tribe of itinerant metalsmiths related to the Midianites and the Israelites.

Kerioth, ancient town in Judea.

Keturah, concubine of Abraham.

Kheresa, ancient village on the E bank of the Sea of Galilee.

Kidron Valley, valley between the Old City of Jerusalem and Mount of Olives.

Kingdom of heaven, spiritual relationship between God and man; spiritual experience having to do with the enthronement of God in the hearts of men; recognition of the fact of the sovereignty of God, belief in the truth of sonship with God and the consequent brotherhood of men; and faith in the effectiveness of the desire to do the will of God.

Kirmeth, trance prophet from Bagdad.

Kish, city-state in Sumeria; center of the Kish confederation.

Koran, [Qur'an; Arabic *Recitation*] sacred scripture of Islam.

Kung Fu-tze, *see* **Confucius**.

Kush, S portion of the ancient region known as Nubia, in NE Africa.

Kyrios, [Greek *Lord*] translation of the Hebrew word Adonai [*My Lord*] in the Septuagint, the Greek version of the Old Testament.

L

Lagash, last Sumerian capital located midway between the Tigris and Euphrates rivers [in SE modern Iraq].

Lake Superior, largest of the five Great Lakes of N America.

Lamech, in Old Testament, father of Noah [2].

Lanaforge, primary Lanonandek; present System Sovereign of Satania.

Lanonandeks, local universe Sons, offspring of the Creator Son and the Creative Spirit; perform mostly the functions of System Sovereigns and Planetary Princes.

Laotta, Nodite woman with whom Adam committed the folly of Eve.

Lao-tse, [Lao-tzu, 6th century BC] first philosopher of Chinese Taoism.

Lapland, region of N Europe largely within the Arctic Circle, stretching across N Norway, Sweden, and Finland and into the Kola Peninsula of Russia.

Larissa, Greek town in N Greece.

Lasea, ancient location on Crete.

Law Forecasters, second group of the supervising seraphim; forecast possible impacts of any proposed enactment on the lives of will creatures.

Lazarus,   1.   Son of Simon from Bethany and friend of Jesus.
  2.   Beggar in the parable about the rich man and the beggar.

League of Nations, organization for international cooperation established at the end of World War I; ceased its activities during World War II.

Leah, daughter of Apostle Philip, prophetess of Hierapolis.

Lebanon Mountains, mountain range extending N to S in Lebanon.

Lebbeus, *see* **Judas Alpheus**.

Lebonah, ancient settlement in Judea.

Legatus, [Latin *deputy*] official who acted as a deputy general to governors of provinces conquered by ancient Rome.

Lemurs, arboreal chiefly nocturnal mammals related to the monkeys but regarded as constituting a distinct superfamily.

Lesser Road, *see* **Hinayana**.

Levant, lands bordering the E shores of the Mediterranian and Aegean seas.

Levite, member of a group of clans of religious functionaries in ancient Israel.

Leviticus (Wayiqra'; Hebrew *And He Called*] third book of the Latin Vulgate Bible.

Liaison Adjusters, Monitors loaned for the temporal lifetimes of their subjects.

Liaison Stabilizers, Morontia Power Supervisors; convert morontia energy into morontia material.

Liberated Adjusters

Liberated Adjusters, Adjusters eternally liberated from the service for the mortals.

Libya, ancient Greek designation for most of North Africa west of the Nile.

Liege, town in E Belgium.

Life, animation of some pattern-configured or otherwise segregated system of energy——material, mindal, or spiritual.

Life Carriers, offspring of a Creator Son, Creative Spirit and an Ancient of Days; engaged in establishing life on the evolutionary worlds.

Lignite, brownish black coal intermediate between peat and bituminous coal.

Limestone, rock that is formed chiefly by accumulation of organic remains and consists mainly of calcium carbonate.

Livias, ancient town in Perea.

Local universe, structural unit of a minor sector in a superuniverse.

Longs Peak, mountain in north-central Colorado, U.S.A.

Lord of Hosts, one of Deity appellations of the Semites.

Lot, nephew of Abraham.

Loyalatia, seraph not mentioned by name in the **Book of Revelation, 19:10**.

Lucifer, Lanonandek Son, number 37 of the primary order; former Sovereign of Satania, mastermind and leader of the system-wide rebellion.

Luke, author of the third Gospel.

Luminous Persons, *here* Paradise Trinity.

Lut, member of the corporeal staff of Prince Caligastia; head of the guardians of health and life.

Lutentia, rebel System Sovereign of Palonia.

Luxor, [ancient Thebes] town in Upper Egypt.

Luz, ancient town in N Galilee.

Lydda, ancient town in Judea.

Lysimachia, ancient town in Thrace, SE Balkans.

M

Macad, ancient town in Perea.

Maccabees, priestly family of Jews who organized a successful rebellion against the Seleucid rulers.

Macedonia, region in the south-central part of the Balkan Peninsula.

Machaerus, ancient settlement and fortress in Perea.

Machiventa Melchizedek, one of the twenty-four counselors; Melchizedek Son incarnated in the flesh on Urantia in the days of Abraham.

Madagascar, island, lying off the SE coast of Africa in the SW Indian Ocean.

Madon, village in Galilee.

Magadan Park, natural park near Bethsaida-Julias.

Magdala, village on the W coast of the Sea of Galilee.

Magellanic Cloud, star cluster of globular type.

Magi, *here* wise men from the East.

Magisterial Sons, [Avonals] Paradise Sons, planetary helpers and judges of the world of space.

Magnetism, *here* magnetic energy.

Mahayana, [Sanskrit *Greater Vehicle*] more liberal and innovative school of Buddhism [cf. **Hinayana**].

Majeston, divine personality created by the Supreme Being in functional liaison with the Deity Absolute; chief of the Reflective Spirits and center for the reflectivity-related activities.

Major sector, app. one tenth of a superuniverse; consists of one hundred minor sectors.

Malach, Syrian believer who met Jesus at Bethsaida and in Phoenicia.

Malachi, [Hebrew *my messenger*] last of the 12 Minor Prophets in the Old Testament.

Malaria, human disease that is caused by sporozoan parasites [genus *Plasmodium*] in the red blood cells.

Malavatia, Melchizedek, sponsor of Paper 43 of *The Urantia Book*.

Malchus, bodyguard of the high priest.

Malta, main island of the small archipelago in the central Mediterranean Sea.

Malvorian, first of the Graduate Guides.

Mammals, backboned animals in which the young are nourished with milk secreted by special glands [*mammae*]of the mother.

Mammon, [Aramaic *riches*] material wealth or possessions esp. as having a debasing influence.

Mamre, site of Abraham's encampment near Hebron.

Mana, among Melanesian and Polynesian peoples, a supernatural force or power that may be ascribed to persons, spirits, or inanimate objects.

Manasseh, king of Judah in the 7th century BC.

Mandrake, Mediterranean herb with ovate leaves, yellowish or purple flowers, and a large forked root traditionally credited with human attributes.

Mangus, centurion of the Roman guard stationed at Capernaum.

Manitou, in the culture of N American Indians, pervasive power in the world that individuals can learn to use in their own behalf.

Manotia, supreme seraphim; associate chief of seraphim on Urantia.

Manovandet, Melchizedek, onetime attached to the planetary receivers of Urantia; presenter of Paper 53 of *The Urantia Book*.

Mansant, one of the twenty-four counselors; spiritual teacher of the post-Planetary Prince age.

Mansion World Teachers, Universe Aids; recruited and glorified cherubim and sanobim. Mansion worlds, seven satellites of the first of encircling worlds of Jerusem; the first training spheres of ascending mortals.

Mansurotia, tertiary Lanonandek; first assistant Sovereign of Satania.

Mantutia, Melchizedek, director of the Nebadon comission which sponsored Part I and Part II of *The Urantia Book*.

Marduk, *see* **Bel-Marduk**.

Mardus, leader of the Cynics of Rome.

Mark, *see* **John Mark**.

Marl, loose or crumbling earthy deposit that contains a substantial amount of calcium carbonate.

Mars,   1.   Ancient Roman deity, god of war.

      2. Fourth major planet from the Sun.

Martha,   1.   Jesus' second sister.

      2. Sister of Mary and Lazarus.

      3. Sister of Mary, Jesus' mother.

      4. Elder sister of Andrew and Piter, member of the women's evangelistic corps.

Mary,   1.   Mother of Jesus.

      2. Sister of Martha and Lazarus.

      3. Mother of the Alpheus twins.

      4. Wife of Clopas and sister of Mary, mother of Jesus.

Mary Mark, mother of John Mark.

Mary Magdalene, member of the women's evangelistic corps.

Master Architects, *see* **Architects of the Master Universe**.

Master Force Organizers, Primary Master Force Organizers transform potential force into primordial force; Associate Master Force Organizers transform primordial force into gravity energy.

Master Physical Controllers, offspring of the Supreme Power Centers, comprises 7 orders chiefly occupied in the adjustment of basic energies undiscovered on Urantia.

Master Sons, *see* **Sovereign Sons**.

Master Spirits, mind sources of the superuniverses; administrators of the grand universe.

Matadormus, Pharisee and member of the Sanhedrin, a believer in Jesus.

Material Sons and Daughters, offspring of the Creator Son; highest type of sex-reproducing beings; function as physical uplifters on the evolutionary worlds.

Matthew Levi, apostle of Jesus.

Matthias, disciple chosen as treasurer to replace Judas Iscariot.

Matter, organized energy which is subject to linear gravity except as it is modified by motion and conditioned by mind.

May Day, in medieval and modern Europe, day [May 1] for traditional springtime celebrations originating in pre-Christian agricultural rituals.

Maypole, ritualistic May tree.

Maza, ancient settlement near Jerusalem.

Mecca, in W Saudi Arabia, the most holy city of Islam, birthplace of the Prophet Muhammad.

Mechanical controllers, Master Physical Controllers; segregate, directionize, and intensificate the physical energies; equalize the pressures of the interplanetary circuits.

Medeba, [Madaba] ancient and modern town in Perea, a Moabite stronghold, later an important Byzantine center.

Media, ancient country of NW Iran, generally corresponding to the modern regions of Azerbaijan, Kurdistan, and parts of Kermanshah.

Mediterranean, areas surrounding the Mediterranean Sea.

Mediterranean Sea, intercontinental sea situated between Europe to the N, Africa to the S, and Asia to the E.

Meganta, school of, unknown Alexandrian school where Rodan taught philosophy.

Megiddo, ancient town in Galilee, overlooking the Plain of Esdraelon [Valley of Jezreel].

Mek, member of the corporeal staff of Prince Caligastia; head of the planetary council on art and science.

Melanesians, population of New Guinea and smaller islands in the SW Pacific Ocean.

Melanin, dark biological pigment [biochrome] found in skin, hair, feathers, scales, eyes, and some internal membranes.

Melchizedek, the world of the Melchizedek Sons, pilot world of the Salvington circuit.

Melchizedek of Salem, *see* **Machiventa Melchizedek**.

Melchizedeks, local universe Sons, offspring of Creator Son, Creative Spirit and Father Melchizedek; serve as teachers and counselors.

Melkarth, Phoenician god, chief deity of Tyre and of two of its colonies, Carthage and Gadir.

Memory of Mercy, tertiary seconaphim; actual and replete living records of the mercy extended to individuals and races by the Infinite Spirit.

Memphis, city and capital of ancient Egypt during the Old Kingdom [c. 2575-c. 2130 BC] located S of the Nile delta.

Mercury, innermost planet of the solar system, named after Roman god of trade and travel.

Mesopotamia, [Greek *Land Between the Rivers*] region between the Tigris and Euphrates in W Asia.

Mesozoic, early land-life era; began 150 million years ago, lasted 100 million years.

Messiah, [Hebrew *anointed*] expected king and deliverer of the Jews.

Messina, capital of Messina province in Sicily, Italy.

Micah, Judean prophet in the last half of the 8th century BC.

Micaiah, prophet of doom in the 9th century BC.

Michal, daughter of King Saul.

Michael of Nebadon, Creator Son of the local universe of Nebadon.

Michaels, *see* **Creator Sons**.

Mid-breathers, atmospheric type; inhabitants of a world with normal-density atmosphere.

Midianites, ancient nomadic Arabian tribes.

Midsoniters, progeny of a Melchizedek life carrier and a Material Daughter; not Adjuster indwelt; can't be reckoned as mortal or immortal.

Midspace zones, relatively quiescent zones separating pervaded and unpervaded space.

Midwayers, [midway creatures] offspring of the planetary biologic uplifters or of their immediate progeny [primary type]; offspring of the modified ascendant-mortal staffs of the Planetary Princes [secondary type]; ministering spirits working in association with the angelic hosts.

Mighty Messengers

Mighty Messengers, Trinitized Sons of Attainment; perfected mortals of supreme personal loyalty; the official observers of the superuniverse government to the local universes and systems.

Milcha, cousin of Apostle Thomas; member of the women's evangelistic corps.

Milky Way, vast starry system; the central nucleus of the superuniverse of Orvonton.

Mind, thinking, perceiving, and feeling mechanism of the human organism; technique whereby spirit realities become experiential to creature personalities; organized consciousness not wholly subject to material gravity.

Mind Planners, third group of the transition ministers; effectively group morontia beings and organize their teamwork on the mansion worlds.

Minerva, Roman goddess of wisdom.

Ming, [1368-1644] Chinese imperial dynasty.

Ministering Daughter, *see* **Creative Spirit.**

Ministering Reserves, seventh group of the transition ministers; help to build up character.

Minor sector, structural unit of a superuniverse comprising 100 local universes.

Miocene, third period of the Cenozoic era; lasted 15 million years.

Miriam, 1. Sister of Moses.
  2. Sister of Jesus.

Mispeh, ancient town in Perea.

Mississippi River, largest river of N America.

Mithra, [Mithras] in ancient Indo-Iranian mythology, the god of the sun, justice, contract, and war.

Mithraism, worship of Mithra, the Indo-Iranian god in pre-Zoroastrian Iran.

Mithras, *see* **Mithra.**

Mo Ti, [Mo-tzu, c. 470-c. 391 BC] Chinese philosopher, challenged Confucianism with fundamental doctrine of universal love, the basis of a religious movement known as Mohism.

Moab, ancient country in the highlands east of the Dead Sea.

Mogul, [Mughal] Muslim dynasty that ruled most of N India from the early 16th to the mid-18th century.

Mohammed, [Muhammad, 570-632] Arab prophet and founder of Islam.

Monmatia, our solar system.

Monogamy, condition or practice of having a single mate during a period of time.

Monospiritism, belief that the spirit world represents only good or evil.

Monota, living, nonspirit energy of Paradise.

Monotheism, doctrine or belief that there is but one God.

Monothetic, containing only one thesis.

Montreal, second largest city of Canada, in SE part of the country.

Moqui, [Hopi] westernmost group of Pueblo Indians in NE Arizona, U.S.A.

Moraine, an area covered by rocks and debris carried down and deposited by a glacier.

Morontia, intermediate level of reality between the material and the spiritual; the state intervening between matter and spirit.

Morontia Companions, Messenger Hosts of Space, offspring of a local universe Mother Spirit; friends and associates of all who live the ascending morontia life.

Morontia Counselors, fourth group of the transition ministers; teach, direct, and counsel the surviving mortals in transit to the higher schools of the system headquarters.

Morontia Power Supervisors, offspring of a local universe Mother Spirit, comprises 7 orders of beings; effect a morontia form of materialization receptive to the superimposition of a controlling spirit.

Morontia Progressors, status of mortals from the mansion worlds to the headquarters of the local universe.

Morontia World, second transition culture world.

Morrison beds, continental clastic wedge of lacustrine and fluvial mudstone, siltstone, sandstone, and conglomerate.

Moses, one of the twenty-four counselors; spiritual leader of the Semites, who led his people out from the Egyptian enslavement.

Most High Assistants, Universe Aids; temporary volunteering representatives of the central and superuniverse to, or observers of, the local creations.

Most Highs, *see* **Constellation Fathers**.

Mota, morontia wisdom, experiential connection between the material and the spiritual levels of the universe.

Mother Spirit, *see* **Creative Spirit**.

Mount Carmel, mountain range, NW Israel; divides the Plain of Esdraelon and the Galilee [east and north] from the coastal Plain of Sharon [south].

Mount Gerizim, mountain in Samaria.

Mount Hermon, snowcapped ridge in N Palestine west of Damascus.

Mount Hood, highest peak in Oregon, U.S.A.

Mount Lebanon, *see* **Lebanon Mountains**.

Mount of Olives, multisummited mile-long ridge just east of the Old City of Jerusalem and separated from it by the Kidron valley.

Mount Rainier, highest mountain in the state of Washington, U.S.A.

Mount Royal, Mountain peak around which the city of Montreal [Canada] was built.

Mount Sartaba, mountain peak in E Galilee overlooking the Jordan valley.

Mount Seraph, highest elevation on Jerusem.

Mountain Shasta, peak of the Cascade Range in the Shasta-Trinity National Forest, N California.

Mount Sinai, granitic peak of the south-central Sinai Peninsula.

Mount Tabor, historic elevation of N Israel, in Lower Galilee.

Mount Zion, easternmost of the two hills of ancient Jerusalem.

Mystery cults, secret cults of the Greco-Roman world that offered to individual initiates a mode of religious experience not provided by the official public religions.

Mystery Monitor, *see* **Thought Adjuster**.

Mysticism, technique of the cultivation of the consciousness of the presence of God; belief that direct knowledge of God, spiritual truth, or ultimate reality can be attained through subjective experience.

N

Nabal, rich Edomite whose widow became the second wife of King David.

Nabon, high priest of Mithraism, who held many talks with Jesus in Rome.

Nabodad, leader of the Salem school at Kish.

Naboth, citizen of Jezreel, a commoner, whose property was taken by King Ahab.

Nabu, [Nebo] major god in the Assyro-Babylonian pantheon, patron of the art of writing and a god of vegetation.

Nebuchadnezzar, [Nebuchadrezzar II, 630-561 BC] second and greatest king of the Chaldean dynasty of Babylonia [reigned c. 605-c. 561 BC].

Nahor, brother of Abraham.

Nain, ancient town in Galilee.

Nalda, Samaritan woman who talked with Jesus at the Jacob's well.

Nambia, first-born Life Carrier of Nebadon.

Nanak, [1469-1539] Indian spiritual teacher, the first guru of the Sikhs, a monotheistic religious group that combines Hindu and Muslim influences.

Naomi, bride at the Cana wedding.

Naples, city in S Italy.

Nasanta, daughter of Elman; member of the women's evangelistic corps.

Nathan,   1.   Greek Jew from Caesarea.
   2. Potter from Nazareth.
   3. Associate of Apostle John who wrote the fourth Gospel.
   4. Messenger from Busiris.

Nathaniel, 1.   Apostle of Jesus.
   2. Wealthy Pharisee from Ragaba.

Nazarite, [Hebrew **nazar** *to abstain from* or *to consecrate oneself to*] sacred person whose separation was marked by his uncut hair and his abstinence from wine; voluntarily vowed to undertake special religious observances.

Neanderthalers, descendants of Badonites; dominated the world for almost half a million years.

Nebadon, local universe, number 84 in the minor sector of Ensa.

Nebadon Corps of Completion, unrevealed corps of the local universe.

Nebula, clouds of gas or dust in interstellar space.

Necho, [Necho II, fl. 7th-6th century BC] king of Egypt [reigned 610-595 BC] and a member of the 26th dynasty.

Necromancy, conjuration of the spirits of the dead for purposes of magically revealing the future or influencing the course of events.

Negativism, attitude of mind marked by skepticism.

Nepal, landlocked country of S Asia.

Neptune, in Roman religion, originally the god of freshwater; later was identified with the Greek Poseidon and thus became a deity of the sea.

Nereids, any of the daughters of the sea god Nereus and of Doris, daughter of Oceanus.

Nerites, ancient nomadic tribes of SW Asia.

New Stone Age, [Neolithic Period] second period of the Stone Age, characterized by ground and polished rock tools and the adoption of a new technique of stoneworking.

Newfoundland, large island in E Canada.

Nicaea, city in Asia Minor.

Nicodemus, member of Sanhedrin who acknowledged his faith in Jesus.

Nicopolis, city in NW Greece.

Nile, river in E Africa, longest in the world.

Nineveh, oldest and most populous city of the ancient Assyrian Empire, situated on the east bank of the Tigris.

Nirvana, [Sanskrit *Extinction* or *Blowing out*] in Indian religious thought, the supreme goal of the meditation disciplines; in Buddhism, the transcendent state of freedom achieved by the extinction of desire and of individual consciousness.

Noah, 1. Member of the Urantia reception committee, the son of the architect and builder of the first Garden.

 2. Wine maker of Aram who built a houseboat.

Nod, member of the corporeal staff; head of the commission on industry and trade; leader of the rebellious members of the corporeal staff of Prince Caligastia.

Nodites, descendants of the 60 rebellious members of the corporeal staff of Prince Caligastia and their 44 modified assistants; the eighth race of Urantia.

Nog, god of light and fire of the lowest types of the Sangik races after the fall of Dalamatia.

Nonbreathers, inhabitants of a world with no atmosphere.

Norana, Syrian woman whose daughter was healed by Jesus.

Nordan the Kenite, disciple of Melchizedek.

Nordics, peoples of N Europe.

Norlatiadek, constellation, number 70 in the local universe of Nebadon.

North Sea, shallow, NE arm of the Atlantic Ocean extending southward from the Norwegian Sea.

O

Obadiah, [Hebrew *servant of Yahweh*] in the Old Testament, one of the Minor Prophets.

Oban, prehistoric settlement in the region of the present Caspian Sea.

Og, Amorite king of Bashan defeated by the Israelites at his frontier town Edrei.

Ohio River, major river artery of the east-central United States.

Okhban, unknown Egyptian prophet.

Old Testament, set of sacred writings shared by Judaism and Christianity.

Old Stone Age, [Paleolithic Period] ancient cultural stage, or level, of human development, characterized by the use of rudimentary chipped stone tools.

Oligocene, second peeriod of the Cenozoic era; lasted 10 million years.

Olivet, *see* **Mount of Olives.**

Olympus, mountain peak, the highest in Greece; in Greek mythology, the abode of gods and the site of the throne of Zeus.

Omen

Omen, occurrence or phenomenon believed to portend a future event.

Omniaphim, angelic order, common offspring of the Infinite Spirit and the Seven Supreme Executives; ministering spirits of the superuniverses.

Omri, [reigned 876-869 or c. 884-c. 872 BC] king of Israel, the father of Ahab.

Onagar, one of the twenty-four counselors; spiritual leader of the pre-Planetary Prince age.

Onamonalonton Hesunanin, one of the twenty-four counselors; spiritual leader of the red man about sixty-five thousand years ago.

One-brained type, first of the three basic organizations of the brain mechanism.

One-Two-Three the First, one of the twenty-four counselors; the leader of the loyal midway creatures at the time of the Caligastia betrayal.

Ophel, district of Jerusalem E of Mt. Zion.

Opossums, American marsupials that usu. have a pointed snout and prehensile tail.

Oracle,   1.   Person through whom a deity is believed to speak.

    2. Shrine in which a deity reveals hidden knowledge or the divine purpose through such a person.

Orange race, one of the three secondary evolutionary races of Urantia; ceased to exist about one hundred thousand years ago.

Ordovician, second period of the Paleozoic era; lasted 50 million years.

Original Son, *see* **Eternal Son.**

Orion, major constellation named for the Greek mythological hunter.

Orlandof, one of the twenty-four counselors; spiritual leader of the blue men.

Orphic brotherhood, religious communities which practiced mystery religion based on the teachings and songs of Orpheus, legendary hero endowed with superhuman musical skills.

Orvonon, one of the twenty-four counselors; spiritual leader of the indigo races.

Orvonton, superuniverse number 7.

Osiris, [Usiri] Egyptian god of fertility, and god of the underworld.

Ovid, Phoenician teacher who proclaimed the Salem doctrines in Ur.

P

Palatine hill, plateau where city of Rome was founded.

Paleozoic, marine-life era; began 400 million years ago, lasted 250 million years.

Palonia, local system in Nebadon where Michael served his bestowal as System Sovereign.

Pandora, [Greek *All-Giving*] in Greek mythology, the first woman; opened the jar ["Pandora's box"] containing all manner of misery and evil, from which the evils flew out over the earth.

Panoptia, planet in Satania.

Pantaenus, one of the leaders of the School of Alexandria, the first Christian institution of higher learning, founded in the mid-2nd century AD.

Pantheism, doctrine that equates God with the forces and laws of the universe.

Pantheon, gods of a people, esp. the officially recognized gods.

Paphos, ancient and modern town in SW Cyprus.

Paradise, *see* **Isle of Paradise.**

Paradise Citizens, beings resident on Paradise.

Paradise Companions, composite group of higher angels; assigned as associates to all classes of beings who may chance to be alone on Paradise.

Paradise Presence, *see* **Deity.**

Paradise Sons of God, offspring of the Paradise Deities; embrace Creator Sons, Magisterial Sons, and Trinity Teacher Sons.

Paradise Trinity, eternal Deity union of the Universal Father, the Eternal Son, and the Infinite Spirit.

Parchment, skin of a sheep or goat prepared for writing on.

Parthia, 1. Ancient land corresponding roughly to the modern region of Khorasan in Iran.

2. Parthian empire [247 BC-AD 224] founded and ruled by the ancient Iranian Arsacid dynasty.

Parsees, [Parsis] descendents of Zoroastrian Iranian (Persian) immigrants in India.

Passover, Jewish holiday beginning on the 14th of the month of Nisan [March or April] and commemorating the Hebrews' liberation from slavery in Egypt.

Patagonia, semiarid scrub plateau in S Argentina.

Paternalism, system under which an authority undertakes to supply needs or regulate conduct of those under its control in matters affecting them as individuals as well as in their relations to authority and to each other.

Patmos, island in Aegean sea, traditional place of exile in ancient Rome.

Patrae, ancient city in Achaea, member of the Achaean League.

Paul of Tarsus, religious philosopher; a key figure in the establishing of the Christian religion.

Peat, partially carbonized vegetable tissue formed by partial decomposition in water of various plants.

Peer, 1. Member of the highest body of constellation legislators.

2. One that is of equal standing with another.

Pella, one of the Decapolis cities east of Jordan.

Penance, 1. Act of self-abasement, mortification, or devotion performed to show sorrow or repentance for sin.

2. Sacramental rite that consists of private confession, absolution, and a penance directed by the confessor.

Pentecost, 1. Jewish religious holiday, 7 weeks after Passover.

2. Day of the coming of the Spirit of Truth on Urantia.

Penuel, ancient town in Perea.

Pepi, third king of the 6th dynasty [c. 2325-c. 2150 BC] of ancient Egypt.

Perea, historical part of Palestine east of the Jordan River.

Perfections of Days, Supreme Trinity Personalities; the rulers of the major sectors of the superuniverses.

Perfectors of Wisdom, Stationary Sons of the Trinity; personification of divine wisdom to the universes.

Permian

Permian, sixth period of the Paleozoic era; lasted 30 million years.

Perpetua, Simon Peter's wife, member of the women's evangelistic corps.

Persia, kingdom of Iran in SW Asia.

Persian peninsula, prehistoric S extension of Mesopotamia.

Personal Aids of the Infinite Spirit, Higher Personalities of the Infinite Spirit; exclusive assistance of the Paradise presence of the Third Person of Deity.

Personality, [of a creature] unique bestowal of the Universal Father; the only changeless reality in the changing creature experience; unifies all other coordinate factors of an individual; distinguished by self-consciousness and relative free will.

Personalized Adjusters, Monitors who have served with the incarnated Paradise Sons, or have achieved unusual distinction during the mortal indwelling, but whose subjects rejected survival; classified as ascending Sons of God.

Personalized Monitors, *see* **Personalized Adjusters**.

Pervaded space, horizontal space of the universes.

Peter, *see* **Simon Peter**.

Phallic cult, religious activities that involve sexuality or the symbolism of the male or female sexual organs.

Pharisees, Jewish religious party that flourished in Palestine during the latter part of the Second Temple period [515 BC-AD 70].

Pharos of Alexandria, one of the Seven Wonders of the World, lighthouse built in about 280 BC on the island of Pharos in the harbor of Alexandria.

Phasaelis, [Phasael] ancient town in central Palestine.

Phenix, ancient settlement on the Isle of Crete.

Philadelphia, [modern Amman] Decapolis city in Perea.

Philanthropy, goodwill to fellowmen; esp. active effort to promote human welfare.

Philip,   1.   Apostle of Jesus.
          2.   *see* **Herod Philip**.

Philistines, people of Aegean origin who settled on the S coast of Palestine in the 12th century BC.

Philo of Alexandria, [Philo Judaeus, 15-10 BC-AD 45-50] religious philosopher; made the first systematic attempt to apply Greek philosophical concepts to Jewish doctrines.

Philosopher's stone, stone that was believed capable of transmuting base metals into gold.

Phoenicia, ancient region corresponding to modern Lebanon, with adjoining parts of modern Syria and Israel.

Phrygia, ancient district in west-central Anatolia.

Phylacteries, square leather boxes containing slips inscribed with scriptural passages.

Phylum, primary division of the animal kingdom.

Physical controllers, nonpersonal regulators of the basic energies unknown on Urantia.

Pikes Peak, peak in the Front Range of the Rocky Mountains in Colorado, U.S.A.

Pilate Pontius, [d. after AD 36] Roman procurator (governor) of Judea, Samaria, and Idumea [AD 26-36] under the emperor Tiberius.

Pindar, [c. 518-442 or 438 BC] lyric poet of ancient Greece.

Pisidia, ancient region of S Asia Minor.

Pitcairn Island, isolated, volcanic formation in the south-central Pacific Ocean.

Placenta, vascular organ in mammals that unites the fetus to the maternal uterus.

Planetary Adams, *see* **Material Sons and Daughters**.

Planetary Custodians, Morontia Power Supervisors; constitute the local planetary council of supreme morontia authority in each morontia world.

Planetary Helpers, fifth seraphic order; 7 groups, primarily assigned to the service of the Planetary Adams.

Planetary Prince, Lanonandek Son; chief administrator of an inhabited world.

Planetary Sovereign, Planetary Prince of the era of light and life.

Planetesimal, small space body.

Plato, [428-348/347 BC] ancient Greek philosopher.

Pleistocene, fifth period of the Cenozoic era; lasted over 2 million years.

Pliocene, fourth period of the Cenozoic era; lasted about 10 million years.

Pole Star, [*also* polestar] brightest star that appears nearest to either celestial pole at any particular time; in N Hemisphere also called North Star; at present the polestar is Polaris.

Polyandry, state or practice of having more than one husband or male mate at one time.

Polygamy, marriage in which a spouse of either sex may have more than one mate at the same time.

Polygyny, state or practice of having more than one wife or female mate at one time.

Polynesia, ethnogeographic grouping of islands scattered across a huge triangular area of the east-central Pacific Ocean.

Porogia, local system in Nebadon.

Porshunta, one of the twenty-four counselors; spiritual leader of the extinct orange race about 300,000 years ago.

Portalon, local universe in Orvonton.

Porphyreon, ancient town on the Phoenician coast.

Potential, realities which carry undisclosed capacity for growth; that which is becoming and will be.

Power centers, manipulators and regulators of the circuits of universe energy; function to downstep and modify these power circuits.

Praetorium, official residence of the governor of a Roman province.

Prajapati, [Sanskrit *Lord of Creatures*] creator figure of the Vedic period of ancient India; in the post-Vedic age came to be identified with Brahma.

Primal Father, *see* **Universal Father**.

Primary Associators, Master Physical Controllers; energy conservators and custodians.

Primary Eventuated Master Force Organizers, beings of unrevealed origin; transmute primordial force into primary energy.

Primary midwayers, offspring of the corporeal stuff of Prince Caligastia.

Primitive man, man before the arrival of the Planetary Prince.

Primordial force

Primordial force, a possible nether Paradise function of the Unqualified Absolute; first basic change in space potency.

Prince of Peace, Paradise bestowal Son on a planetary mission.

Prince of Salem, *see* **Machiventa Melchizedek**.

Priscilla, wife and companion of Aquila.

Procurator, officer of the Roman empire entrusted with management of the financial affairs of a province and often having administrative powers as agent of the emperor.

Progressor, classification of mortals from the mansion worlds on up through the spheres of the system, constellation, and the universe.

Prometheus, [Greek *Forethinker*] in Greek religion, one of the Titans, the supreme trickster, and a god of fire.

Promiscuity, casual, irregular sexual behavior, not restricted to one sexual partner.

Propitiate, gain or regain the favor or goodwill of.

Proterozoic, life-dawn era; began 550 million years ago, lasted 150 million years.

Protoplasm, organized colloidal complex of organic and inorganic substances [as proteins and water] that constitutes the living nucleus, cytoplasm, plastids, and mitochondria of the cell.

Protozoa, motile and heterotrophic unicellular protists.

Providence, divine guidance or care; God conceived as the power sustaining and guiding human destiny.

Psalmist, *here* author of the Book of Psalms.

Pterosaurs, extinct flying reptiles with a featherless wing membrane extending from the side of the body along the arm to the end of the greatly elongated fourth digit.

Ptolemaic dynasty, independent kingship in Egypt between 305-30 BC.

Ptolemais, coastal city of ancient Cyrenaica (now part of Libya); received its name from Ptolemy III.

Puberty, condition of being or the period of becoming first capable of reproducing sexually.

Puget Sound, deep inlet of the eastern North Pacific indenting NW Washington state, U.S.A.

Puissant energy, first phase of the transmutation of primordial force.

Punjab, historical region in S Asia.

Pure energy, *see* **primordial force**.

Purim, [Hebrew *Lots*] joyous Jewish festival commemorating the survival of the Jews who, in the 5th century BC, were marked for death by their Persian rulers.

Purple, *here* purple robe worn as an emblem of rank or authority.

Pygmies, subgroup, roughly corresponding to a breeding isolate in genetics, of the Negroid [African] geographic race.

Q

Quadrillion, *here* figure 1 followed by 15 zeroes (10^{15}).

Quadruped, having four feet.

Qualified Absolute, *see* **Deity Absolute**.

Qualified Vicegerents of the Ultimate, unrevealed order.

Quantum [*pl.* quanta] any of the very small increments or parcels into which many forms of energy are subdivided.

Quarantine, state of enforced isolation.

Quebec, E province of Canada.

Queensland, state of NE Australia, occupying the wettest and most tropical part of the continent.

Quickeners of Morality, fourth group of the administrator seraphim; teach the fruitfulness of patience.

Quinine, bitter crystalline alkaloid from cinchona bark.

R

Rachel,　1.　Cousin and wife of Jacob (*see* **Jacob, 1**).

　　2.　Sister-in-law of Jude, brother of Jesus; member of the women's evangelistic corps.

Racial interpreters, second group of the transition ministers; further the efforts of the race commissioners to harmonize the varied viewpoints of the races.

Ragaba, ancient town in Perea.

Rainier, *see* **Mount Rainier**.

Ramah, ancient town in Galilee.

Ramath, ancient town in Perea.

Ramman, [also, Had, Hadda, Haddu, Rimmon] West Semitic god of storms, thunder, and rain; the chief baal ["lord"] of the West Semites.

Rantowoc, first mortal, of the red race, to receive a personal guardian.

Rantulia, local system in Nebadon.

Ratta, wife of Adamson.

Rebecca,　1.　Daughter of Ezra (*see* **Ezra, 2**).

　　2.　Daughter of Joseph of Arimathea; member of the women's evangelistic corps.

Recents of Days, Supreme Trinity Personalities; rulers of the minor sectors of the superuniverses.

Recorder-Teachers, sixth group of the transition ministers; recorders of the borderland transactions of the spiritual and the physical.

Recorders, 1.　Sixth group of the supreme seraphim.

　　2.　Sixth group of the superior seraphim.

　　3.　Sixth group of the supervisor seraphim.

　　4.　Sixth group of the administrator seraphim.

　　5.　Sixth group of the planetary helpers.

Red race, one of the three primary evolutionary races of Urantia.

Reflective Image Aids, 49 creations of the Reflective Spirits; duplicate the Reflective Spirits in everything except the phenomenon of reflectivity.

Reflective Spirits, 49 beings of Trinity origin united in the groups of 7; reflect the natures and characters of the seven possible combinations of the association of the divinity characteristics of the Universal Father, the Eternal Son, and the Infinite Spirit.

Reflectivity, *see* **universe reflectivity**.

Remona, wife of Cain.

Resting stage, [diapause] period of physiologically enforced dormancy between periods of activity.

Revealed religion, universe attitude which is a spirit derivative; the assurance of, and belief in, the conservation of eternal realities, the survival of personality, and the eventual attainment of the cosmic Deity.

Revelation, act of revealing or communicating divine truth.

Reversion directors, courtesy colony; promoters of relaxation, ministers of the exalted humor of the morontia and spirit realms.

Rhodes, island in Greece, the largest of the Dodecanese group, and the most easterly in the Aegean Sea.

Rig-Veda, in Hinduism, a collection of 1028 hymns dating from second millennium BC.

Rimmon, ancient town in Galilee.

Rocky Mountains, mountain range, a major component of the great upland system of W North America, extending from Canada through the W United States to Mexico.

Roman Empire, [27 BC-AD 476] lands and peoples subject to the authority of ancient Rome.

Rome, historic city and capital of Italy, on the Tiber River, in central Italy.

Romulus (and Remus), legendary founders of Rome. As infants, they were ordered drowned in the Tiber, but the trough in which they were placed floated down the river and came to rest at the site of the future Rome.

Ruben, [Reuben] one of the tribes of Israel, named after the oldest of Jacob's sons born of Leah, his first wife.

Rufus, injured lad from Cyrene, who received first aid from Jesus; son of Simon (*see* **Simon, 5**)

Ruth,   1.   One of the ancestors of Mary, mother of Jesus.

    2.   Sister of Jesus.

    3.   Eldest daughter of Matthew Levi, member of the women's evangelistic corps.

Ryonin, evangelistic monk of the Buddhist Tendai sect in the early 12th century.

S

Sabbath, seventh day of the week observed from Friday evening to Saturday evening as a day of rest and worship by Jews and some Christians.

Sadducees, conservative and static party, consisted mainly of the old priesthood and landed aristocracy; collaborators with Rome.

Sadib, tertiary Lanonandek; second assistant Sovereign of Satania.

Safed, [Zefat] town in Galilee.

Sagittarius, star cloud around which the local universe of Nebadon moves.

Sakyamuni, *see* **Gautama Siddhartha.**

Salamis, principal city of ancient Cyprus, located on the east coast of the island.

Salem, ancient settlement on the site of the later Jerusalem.

Salemites, preachers from Salem, followers of the doctrines of Machiventa Melchizedek.

Salome,   1.   Sister of Mary, mother of Jesus.
    2. Wife of Zebedee.

Salsatia, Nebadon Census Director.

Salvington, headquarters of the local universe of Nebadon.

Samaria,   1.   Central region of ancient Palestine.
    2. Ancient town in central Palestine.

Samson, Israelite hero and a legendary warrior of the tribal period of Israel in Canaan [1200-1000 BC].

Samuel, [11th century BC] religious hero of Israel, seer, priest, judge, prophet.

Sanctities of Service, tertiary seconaphim; reveal the real nature and hidden motives of any service.

Sandmatia, local system in Nebadon.

Sandstone, sedimentary rock consisting of quartz sand united by some cement.

Sangik races, 6 colored races of Urantia, 3 primary and 3 secondary.

Sanhedrin, [synedrion; Greek *counci*] Great Sanhedrin, supreme Jewish legislative and judicial court in Jerusalem under Roman rule.

Sanobim, angelic order, offspring of a Universe Mother Spirit; ministering spirits of the local universes, assistants of seraphim.

Sansa, daughter of Adam and Laotta.

Sanselon, local universe in Orvonton.

Sarah, wife of Abraham.

Sarepta, unknown ancient settlement in Phoenicia.

Sargan, chief of the N blue races.

Sargon,   1.   Priest of Kish in the 3rd millennium BC; united part of Mesopotamia into Kish confederation.
    2. King of Assyria; carried away and into captivity over twenty-five thousand Jews about 700 BC.

Sarid, ancient and modern settlement in Galilee.

Satan, primary Lanonandek; first assistant of Lucifer.

Satania, system of inhabited worlds, number 24, in the constellation of Norlatiadek.

Satisfaction of Service, secondary seconaphim; enhance the value of service and augment the satisfactions to be derived therefrom.

Sato, leader of the group of progenitors of the ancient Greeks, a descendant of Adamson and Ratta.

Saturn, sixth planet from the Sun; named after the Roman god of agriculture.

Saul, first king of Israel [c. 1021-1000 BC].

Scotland, component country of the United Kingdom.

Scythopolis

Scythopolis, [modern Bet She'an] one of the Decapolis cities in Palestine.

Sea of Galilee, [also lake Tiberias, Yam Kinneret] lake in Israel through which the Jordan River flows.

Sea of glass, circular crystal; serves as the receiving area of some architectural spheres as well as for modifying the currents of space and for adapting incoming physical-energy streams.

Sebaste, [Samaria] ancient town in central Palestine.

Seconaphim, angelic order, children of the Reflective Spirits; ministering spirits of the superuniverses.

Second Source and Center, *see* **Eternal Son.**

Secondary Dissociators, Master Physical Controllers; possess enormous anti-gravity endowment and the power of evolving limitless supplies of energy.

Secondary midwayers, offspring of Adamson and Ratta.

Secoraphic, pertaining to seconaphim.

Secret of Greatness and Soul of Goodness, tertiary seconaphim; functionally interdependent; reflect greatness and goodness of any being.

See Fuch, city in Kiangsu province of China.

Segregata, Uversa appellation for primordial force.

Segub, son of Hiel of Bethel; sacrificed in building the walls of Jericho.

Selah, expression occurring in the Psalms and thought to be a liturgical or musical direction.

Seleucid kingdom, [312-64 BC] ancient empire founded by Seleucus I Nicator; at its greatest extent stretched from Thrace in Europe to the border of India.

Selective Assorters, Morontia Power Supervisors; keep morontia beings in progressive synchrony with the morontia life.

Selta, [2nd century AD] author of a Jewish apocalypse who served at the court of Caligula.

Semites, peoples of ancient SW Asia including the Akkadians, Phoenicians, Hebrews, and Arabs.

Sepharvites, citizens of Sepharvaim, ancient town in Assyria.

Sepphoris, ancient capital of Galilee.

Serapatatia, leader of the Syrian Nodites; associate chairman of the Edenic commission on tribal relations.

Seraphic Corps of Completion, seraphic corps on Paradise.

Seraphic Evangels, first group of the transition ministers; help ascending creatures to choose wisely among the optional routes to Edentia, Salvington, Uversa, and Havona.

Seraphim, angelic order, offspring of a Universe Mother Spirit; ministering spirits of the local universes.

Seraphim of the Future, seventh seraphic order; engaged in pursuits relevant to the age of light and life in Nebadon.

Seraphington, one of the Paradise satellites; sacred world of the Father, the "bosom of the Son and the Spirit"; among other secrets, contains the mystery of seraphic transport.

Set, [*also* Seth] ancient Egyptian god, patron of the 11th nome, or province, of Upper Egypt.

Seth, son of Adam and Eve born in the second garden; head of the new priesthood of the garden.

Sethard, unknown religous teacher.

Sethites, new priesthood of the second garden; performed threefold duties of priests, physicians, and teachers.

Sevenfold Deity, *see* **God the Sevenfold**.

Shale, fissile rock that is formed by the consolidation of clay, mud, or silt, has a finely stratified or laminated structure, and is composed of minerals essentially unaltered since deposition.

Shalmaneser III, king of Assyria [reigned 858-824 BC].

Shaman, priest or priestess who uses magic for the purpose of curing the sick, divining the hidden, and controlling events.

Shamash [Sumerian *Utu*] in Mesopotamian religion, the god of the sun, who, with the moon god, Sin and Ishtar, the goddess of Venus, was part of an astral triad of divinities.

Shang-ti, supreme god of the ancient Chinese.

Shasta, *see* **Mount Shasta**.

Shawnee, Algonkian-speaking N American Indian tribe.

Shechem, ancient Canaanite city in central Palestine.

Shekel, 1. Unit of value based on a shekel weight of gold or silver [Hebrew unit is equal to about 252 troy grains].

2. Coin weighing one shekel.

Shekinah, (*also* Shekhina; Hebrew *Dwelling* or *Presence*] in Jewish theology, the presence of God in the world.

Shema, [Hebrew *hear*] the Jewish confession of faith made up of three scriptural texts.

Shemer, [Hebrew *guard*] owner of the land property in central Palestine purchased from him by King Omri.

Shensi, province in NW China.

Sheol, [in the Greek Old Testament, Hades] dwelling place of the dead.

Shiloh, Canaanite town that became the central sanctuary site of the Israelite confederacy during the period of the judges [12th-11th century BC].

Shin, [**Jodo Shinshu**; Japanese *True Pure Land sect*] the largest of the Japanese Buddhist Pure Land sects.

Shinran, [1173-1263] Buddhist philosopher and religious reformer, founder of True Pure Land sect.

Shinto, [Japanese *way of deity*] religious beliefs and practices of Japan.

Shittim, ancient town NE of the Dead Sea.

Shunem, ancient village in Galilee.

Siam, [now Thailand] country in the west of the Indochinese Peninsula of SE Asia.

Sibmah, ancient town in Perea.

Sicilian Bay, Permian bay in the Mediterranean Sea.

Sicily, island of Italy, the largest in the Mediterranean Sea.

Siddim, valley in Judea.

Sidon, ancient and modern city on the Mediterranean coast of Lebanon.

Sierra Nevada

Sierra Nevada,   1. Mountain range in E California.

2. Mountain range in S Spain.

Sierras, *see* **Sierra Nevada.**

Significance of Origins, tertiary seconaphim; living reference genealogies of the grand universe beings.

Sikhism, religion of an Indian group founded in the Punjab in the late 15th century AD by Guru Nanak.

Silas, [Saint Silvanus] early Christian prophet and missionary, companion of Apostle Paul.

Siloam, spring and pool near Jerusalem.

Silurian, third period of the Paleozoic era; lasted 25 million years.

Simeon,   1.   Judean singer who performed a poem written in honor of baby Jesus.

2. Second son born to Jacob and Leah.

Simon,   1.   Brother of Jesus.

2. Father of Mary, Martha, and Lazarus.

3. Uncle of Jesus.

4. Leather merchant from Mesopotamia.

5. Influential Pharisee of Jerusalem.

6. Cyrenian who bore the cross of Jesus.

7. Citizen of Bethphage, who harbored Thomas after the crucifixion of Jesus.

8. Leading citizen of Bethany after the death of Simon, father of Mary, Martha, and Lazarus.

Simon Peter, apostle of Jesus.

Simon Zelotes, apostle of Jesus.

Sin, deliberate disloyalty to Deity, conscious and wholehearted identification with evil, purposeful resistance to divine reality——a conscious choosing to oppose spiritual progress.

Sinai,   1. *see* **Mount Sinai.**

2. Triangular peninsula linking Africa with Asia.

Singlangton, one of the twenty-four counselors; the first monotheistic teacher of the yellow men about 100,000 years ago; proclaimed the worship of the "One Truth".

Sinkiang, Chinese name for the E Turkestan.

Sisera, commander in chief of the forces of Jabin, a king of Hanaan, defeated by Deborah and Barak.

Siva, [*also* Shiva; Sanskrit *Auspicious One*] one of the main deities of Hinduism; lord of life and death, god of fertility, and master of destruction.

Siwalik Hills, sub-Himalayan mountain range.

Skeptics, philosophical attitude of doubting the knowledge claims set forth in various areas; Greek Skepticism was founded by Pyrrhon of Elis (c. 360-c. 272 BC).

Social Architects, third group of the supervisor seraphim; enhance all sincere social contacts on all levels in the local universe.

Socrates, [469?-399 BC] Athenian philosopher, the first of the great trio of ancient Greeks——Socrates, Plato, and Aristotle.

Sodium chloride, [table salt] chemical compound consisting of equal numbers of sodium and chlorine atoms.

Sodom and Gomorrah, ancient towns near the S end of the Dead Sea in Palestine; presumably devastated about 1900 BC by an earthquake in the Dead Sea area.

Solemnity of Trust, tertiary seconaphim; portray the sense of the obligation, sacredness, and solemnity of trust; reflect the trustworthiness of any candidate for confidence or trust.

Solitarington, one of the Paradise satellites; sacred world of the Father, the "bosom of the Father and the Spirit"; holds the secrets of the personal relation of the Infinite Spirit with certain of his higher offspring.

Solitary Messengers, Higher Personalities of the Infinite Spirit; provide personal contact with creations of time and space; function throughout the master universe.

Solomon, [mid-10th century BC] son and successor of David; traditionally regarded as the greatest king of Israel.

Solonia, seraphim, Voice of the Garden.

Soma, personified deity in Indian religion, the "master of plants," the healer of disease, and the bestower of riches.

Somme, river in N France.

Sonarington, one of the Paradise satellites; sacred world of the Father, the "bosom of the Son"; contains the secret of the incarnation of the divine Sons.

Son-Spirit Ministers, first group of the supreme seraphim; assigned to the service of the high Sons and Spirit-origin beings in the local universe.

Sonta-an, ["loved by mother"] Andon's self-given name.

Sontad, first child of Andon and Fonta.

Sonta-en, ["loved by father"] Fonta's self-given name.

Sortoria, local system in Nebadon.

Soul, experiential morontial reality acquired in cooperation of inner spirit with mind; a spiritual and potentially immortal counterpart of character and identity.

Souls of Peace, third group of the planetary helpers; foster peaceful coexistence among planetary races.

Souls of Philosophy, secondary seconaphim; reflect the wisdom of divinity and the philosophy of Paradise.

South Dakota, constituent state of the U.S.A., in the western NC region of the country.

Sovereign Sons, [Master Sons] sevenfold bestowal Creator Sons.

Space potency, free space presence of the Unqualified Absolute.

Space respiration, cyclic expansions and contractions of space.

Spikenard, fragrant ointment of the ancients.

Spirit,   1.   *see* **Thought Adjuster.**

    2.   Highest prepersonal or personal reality.

Spirit Coordinators, third group of superior seraphim; prepare the ascendant creatures for the status of newborn spirit beings.

Spirit of counsel, adjutant mind-spirit.

Spirit of courage, adjutant mind-spirit.

Spirit of intuition, adjutant mind-spirit.

Spirit of knowledge, adjutant mind-spirit.

Spirit of Truth, spirit of Michael of Nebadon on Urantia.

Spirit of understanding, adjutant mind-spirit.

Spirit of wisdom, adjutant mind-spirit.

Spirit of worship, adjutant mind-spirit.

Spiritington, one of the Paradise satellites; sacred world of the Father, the "bosom of the Spirit"; contains the mysteries of reflectivity.

Spiritism, [spiritualism]   1.   Belief that spirits of the dead communicate with the living usu. through a medium.

    2.   View that spirit is a prime element of reality.

Spirits of Brotherhood, second group of the planetary helpers; foster the spirit of brotherhood among planetary races.

Spirits of the Circuits, joint impersonal representation of the Infinite Spirit and the Seven Master Spirits to the seven circuits of the central universe.

Spirits of Trust, fourth group of the planetary helpers; inculcate trust into the minds of evolving men.

Spironga, offspring of the Bright and Morning Star and the Father Melchizedek; the spirit helpers of the local universe.

Spitzbergen, [Spitsbergen] archipelago in the Arctic Ocean.

Spornagia, high order of animal life on the headquarters worlds of the local universe; upkeep material life and afford physical ministry to all orders of universe personalities requiring material service.

Splandon, major sector number 5 of the superuniverse of Orvonton.

Star drifts, whirl of the major sectors about the superuniverse headquarters.

Star Students, courtesy colony; celestial astronomers.

Stationary Sons of the Trinity, generic name for Perfectors of Wisdom, Divine Counselors, Universal Censors, and the seven orders of Supreme Trinity Personalities.

St. Croix, valley in Wisconsin, U.S.A.

St. Lawrence, great hydrographic system of east-central N America.

Stephen, Hellenist Jew and Christian deacon in Jerusalem; the first Christian martyr.

Stoics, adherents of the Stoic school of philosophy; originated in the views of Socrates and Plato, as modified by Zeno and Chrysippus in the 3rd century BC; taught that men should be free from passion and submit without complaint to necessity.

Stone of Scone, [*also* Stone of Destiny] rectangular block of pale yellow sandstone associated with the crowning of Scottish kings; in 1296, was taken to England and later placed under the Coronation Chair.

Stonehenge, monumental circular setting of large standing stones surrounded by a circular earthwork, built in prehistoric times beginning about 3100 BC and located in Wiltshire, Eng.

Strait of Gibraltar, channel connecting the Mediterranean Sea with the Atlantic Ocean, lying between southernmost Spain and northwesternmost Africa.

Stratosphere, upper portion of the atmosphere, a nearly isothermal layer that is located above the troposphere.

Student Visitors, courtesy colony; celestial visitors of the universe passing through the various headquarters worlds.

Subbreathers, atmospheric type; inhabitants of a world with low-density atmosphere.

Succoth, ancient town in Perea.

Sudna, Havona Servital.

Suduanism, *see* **Jainism**.

Suez Canal, sea-level waterway separating Africa from Asia.

Suites, ancient tribes of N Mesopotamia.

Sumer,   1.   Ancient region in the southernmost part of Mesopotamia between the Tigris and the Euphrates rivers.

      2. Ancient city-state in Mesopotamia.

Sumeria, *see* **Sumer, 1**.

Suntites, unknown Asian tribes.

Superacting Adjusters, Monitors who have fulfilled their tasks and await the dissolution of the material body or the translation of the immortal soul of their mortal ward.

Superangel World, fourth transitional culture world.

Superangels, *see* **Brilliant Evening Stars**.

Superbreathers, atmospheric type; inhabitants of a world with high-density atmosphere.

Superior seraphim, second seraphic order; 7 groups, perform different functions in local universes.

Supernaphim, angelic order; offspring of the Infinite Spirit [primary], the Master Spirits [secondary], and the Spirits of the Circuits [tertiary]; ministering spirits of the central universe.

Superuniverse, one of the seven structural units of the grand universe.

Superuniverse confederation, union of the perfected local universes of a superuniverse.

Supervising Assistants, first group of the supervising seraphim; helpers of the Most Highs, primarily concerned with the unification and stabilization of a whole constellation.

Supervisor seraphim, third seraphic order; 7 groups, perform different functions in constellations.

Supremacy, functional level of Deity pertaining to finite reality.

Supreme, *see* **God the Supreme**.

Supreme Adjusters, Monitors whose human wards declined eternal survival; subsequently assigned to other mortals.

Supreme Being, unification of three phases of Deity reality, God the Supreme, the Almighty Supreme, and the Supreme Mind.

Supreme Mind, unifyer of power and personality attributes of the Supreme Being.

Supreme Center Supervisors, seven coordinates and associates of the Supreme Power Directors; the regulators of the master energy circuits of the grand universe.

Supreme Council of Destiny, presiding heads of the seven finaliter corps on Paradise.

Supreme Creators, *see* **God the Sevenfold**.

Supreme Executives

Supreme Executives, Supreme Spirits; trinitized by the Father, Son, and Spirit in accordance with the specifications of the Seven Master Spirits; administrative co-ordinators of the grand universe.

Supreme Power Centers, common offspring of the Seven Master Spirits and the Seven Supreme Power Directors; directing centers of the universe power system.

Supreme Power Directors, offspring of the Seven Master Spirits; regulators of physical energy in the grand universe.

Supreme Rulers, undefined group of divine personalities presiding over the destinies of the master universe.

Supreme Seraphim, first seraphic order; 7 groups, closely associated with the Seraphic Corps of Completion.

Supreme Spirit Groups, universal coordinating directors of the seven-segmented administration of the grand universe.

Supreme Trinity Personalities, first seven orders of Stationary Sons of the Trinity.

Supreme-Ultimate, final finite integration of the Supreme and the Ultimate, association of subabsolute and derived Deity.

Suzerainty, dominion of a suzerain, overlordship.

Susa, [*also* Shushan, Susiane, Shush] capital of Elam [Susiana] and administrative capital of king Darius I and his successors from 522 BC.

Susanna, 1. Daughter of the chazan of the Nazareth synagogue and member of the women's evangelistic corps.

   2. Daughter of Ezra of Alexandria.

Susatia, citizens of Salvington, offspring of the Creator Son and Creative Spirit; closely associated with the Spirit-fused mortals of the Nebadon Corps of Perfection.

Susquehanna River, one of the longest rivers of the Eastern Seaboard of the United States.

Sycamore, 1. Fig tree of Africa and the Middle East [the sycamore of Scripture] inferior to the common fig.

   2. Eurasian maple.

Sychar, ancient town in Samaria.

Syracuse, chief Greek city of ancient Sicily.

Syria, country on the E coast of the Mediterranean Sea on the SW fringe of the Asian continent.

System, [of inhabited worlds] basic structural unit of a constellation.

System Coordinators, Morontia Power Supervisors; harmonize and blend differing power systems into a working unit for the associated spheres of any particular group.

System Sovereign, ruler of a local system.

T

Taanach, ancient town in Samaria.

Tabamantia, agondonter of finaliter status; chief of universe directors who inspect experimental worlds of Satania.

Talisman, object held to act as a charm to avert evil and bring good fortune.

Talmai, unknown king of Geshur.

Tamar, one of the ancestors of Mary, mother of Jesus.

Tao, [Chinese *road* or *way*] in Chinese philosophy, a fundamental concept signifying "the correct way," or "Heaven's way."

Taoism, Chinese mystical philosophy traditionally founded by Lao-tzu in the 6th century BC that teaches conformity to the Tao by unassertive action and simplicity.

Tarentum, ancient city in S Italy.

Tarichea, ancient town in Galilee.

Tarim, river in the W China.

Tarshish, unknown location; probably identical with Tarsus in Asia Minor or Tartessus in Spain; other options refer to lands E. of Palestine.

Tarsus, ancient and modern city in south-central Turkey.

Tasmania, island off the SE corner of Australia.

Teaching Counselors, fourth group of the supreme seraphim; assistants of the spiritual teaching corps of the local universe.

Technical Advisers, Messenger Hosts of Space; function in the field of applied law.

Technicians, fifth group of the transition ministers; help new ascenders adjust to the environment of the morontia spheres.

Teherma, Persian businessman, believer in Jesus.

Temple of New Life, resurrection hall on the first mansion world of Satania.

Tenskwatawa, [Laulewasikau] Shawnee Indian chief known as the Prophet.

Terah, father of Abraham.

Tertiaphim, angelic order, offspring of the Infinite Spirit; ministering spirits of the superuniverses.

Tetrarch, governor of the fourth part of a province.

Thaddeus, *see* **James Alpheus**.

Thamna, ancient town in central Palestine.

Thapsacus, ancient town on the Euphrates River.

Thebes, [modern Luxor] capital of the ancient Egyptian empire at its heyday.

Third Source and Center, *see* **Infinite Spirit**.

Thomas Didymus, apostle of Jesus.

Thor,   1.   Commander of Andites in the final battle of the Somme.

    2.   Deity common to all the early Germanic peoples.

Those High in Authority, Trinitized Sons of Attainment; perfected mortals with superior administrative ability; serve as executives of the Ancients of Days.

Those Without Name and Number, Trinitized Sons of Attainment; perfected mortals with superior judicial ability.

Thoth, [Egyptian *Djhuty, Djhowtey*] in Egyptian religion, a god of the moon, of reckoning, of learning, and of writing.

Thought Adjusters, prepersonal fragments of the Universal Father; represent the Universal Father to the mortal creatures of time and space; elevate the mortal minds and translate the immortal souls of men up to the levels of Paradise perfection; sojourn in the human mind.

Thought Changer, designation of a Thought Adjuster from the arrival to comparative full growth of a human ward.

Thought Controller

Thought Controller, designation of a Thought Adjuster from the attainment of discretion to deliverance from the flesh of the human ward.

Thought recorders, specialized group of celestial artisans; preserve and reproduce the superior thought of the realms.

Thrace, ancient and modern region of the SE Balkans.

Three-brained type, third of the three basic organizations of the brain mechanism.

Thunderstones, rock melted and crystallized as a result of a lightning stroke.

Tiber, river in Europe, second longest in Italy.

Tiberias, city in Galilee, on the W shore of the Sea of Galilee.

Tiberius, [Tiberius Caesar Augustus, 42 BC-AD 37] second Roman emperor [AD 14-37] adopted son of Augustus.

Tibet, [Bod] historic region and autonomous region of China that is often referred to as "the roof of the world."

Tiglath, youth who accompanied Jesus on the way to Mt. Hermon.

Tigris, river in SW Asia.

Timothy, disciple of Apostle Paul, whom he accompanied on his missions.

Ti Tao, mountain pass in NW China.

Titus, 1. Roman commander and the conqueror of Jerusalem in AD 70, Roman emperor [AD 79-81].
>   2. Disciple of Apostle Paul, for whom he was secretary.
>   3. Prominent citizen of Capernaum, believer in Jesus.

Toda, pastoral tribe of the Nilgiri Hills of S India.

Todan, gospel messenger in Mesopotamia and beyond.

Tom-tom, long and narrow small-headed drum commonly beaten with the hands.

Totem, object serving as the emblem of a family or clan and often as a reminder of its ancestry.

Town of Judah, ancient town in Judea close to Jerusalem.

Tranosta, Uversa appellation for transcendental energy.

Transcendental, 1. Timeless.
>   2. Precreative.
>   3. Pertaining to the ultimate level of existence.

Transcendental energy, energy system of the upper Paradise.

Transcendentalers, absonite "eventuators" of the central universe; neither creators nor creatures.

Transcendental Recorders, unrevealed personal beings able to traverse gravity.

Transitional culture spheres, seven major satellites of Jerusem.

Transition Ministers, sixth seraphic order; 7 groups, contribute to creature transition from the material to the spiritual estate.

Transporters, 1. Fifth group of the superior seraphim.
>   2. Fifth group of the supervisor seraphim.
>   3. Fifth group of the administrator seraphim.
>   4. Fifth group of the planetary helpers.

Tree of life, shrub of Edentia, which stored up certain space-energies antidotal to aging; appeared on Urantia with the arrival of Caligastia; destroyed after the fall of the first Garden.

Triad, union or group of three.

Triassic, first period of Mesozoic era; extended over 25 million years.

Triata, Uversa appellation for Havona energy.

Trillion, *here* thousand billions [10^{12}].

Trilobites, extinct Paleozoic marine arthropods having the segments of the body divided by furrows on the dorsal surface into three lobes.

Trimurti, in Hinduism, a triad of the three great gods, Brahma, Vishnu, and Shiva.

Trinitarian, of or relating to a trinity.

Trinitization, 1. Threefold Deity personalization.

    2. Method of creating new beings by Paradise Deities, investing with authority to represent the Trinity.

    3. Method of creating new beings by glorified creatures of Paradise-Havona.

Trinitized Ambassadors, Trinitized Sons of Selection; assist Ancients of Days in dealings with problems involving the Son-fused order of personality.

Trinitized Custodians, Trinitized Sons of Selection; Trinity-embraced seraphim and midwayers; officers of the superuniverse governments who administer group affairs and foster collective projects.

Trinitized Secrets of Supremacy, Stationary Sons of the Trinity; supreme and ultimate administrators, directors of the Paradise worlds of the Father.

Trinitized Sons of Attainment, Trinitized Sons of God; embrace Mighty Messengers, Those High in Authority, and Those without Name and Number.

Trinitized Sons of Destiny, Trinitized Sons of God; joint creations of finaliters and Paradise-Havoners.

Trinitized Sons of Perfection, Trinitized Sons of God; embrace Celestial Guardians and High Son Assistants.

Trinitized Sons of Selection, Trinitized Sons of God; embrace Trinitized Custodians and Trinitized Ambassadors.

Trinity, *see* **Paradise Trinity**.

Trinity of Trinities, existential-experiential Trinity Infinite, unification of The Paradise Trinity, The Ultimate Trinity and The Absolute Trinity; possibly equivalate to the person of the Universal Father on the level of the I AM; final expression of all that is implied in triunities and associated triodities.

Trinity of Ultimacy, *see* **Ultimate Trinity**.

Trinity Teacher Sons, [Daynals] supreme co-ordinating personalities of Trinity origin; the supernal teachers of all personalities.

Triodity, a triune relationship which is non-Father in constitution and involved in the cosmic appearance of experiential Deities.

Triunity, one of the seven functional unions of the Absolutes.

Troas, [*also* Troad] the land of Troy [ancient city in NW Asia Minor], ancient district formed mainly by the NW projection of Asia Minor into the Aegean Sea.

Troposphere, lowest region of the atmosphere.

Tubal-Cain, son of Lamech and his second wife, Zillah.

Turanians, any of the various peoples speaking Ural-Altaic languages.

Turkestan, historical region in Central and Middle Asia.

Tut

Tut, member of the corporeal staff of Prince Caligastia; head of the governors of advanced tribal relations.

Tutankhamen, [Tutankhaten, *also* Nebkheperura] king of Egypt of the 18th dynasty.

Two-brained type, second of the three basic organizations of the brain mechanism.

Tyrannus, school of, unknown school in Ephesus where Paul conducted lectures on religion and philosophy.

Tyre, coastal town in S Lebanon; a major Phoenician seaport in the ancient times.

Tyrian purple, crimson or purple dye that is related to indigo, obtained by the ancient Greeks and Romans from gastropod mollusks.

Tyrus, ancient town in Perea.

U

Ultimata, Uversa appellation for puissant and gravity energies.

Ultimate, *see* **God the Ultimate**.

Ultimate Trinity, Supreme Being, Supreme Creator Personalities, and Architects of the Master Universe.

Ultimaton, basic unit of materialized energy, the first measurable form of energy.

Umajor the fifth, headquarters of the major sector, Splandon.

Uminor the third, headquarters of the minor sector, Ensa.

Unattached Ministers, seventh group of the supreme seraphim.

Unions of Days, Supreme Trinity Personalities; Paradise representatives in the local universes.

Unions of Souls, secondary seconaphim; reflect the ideals and status of ethical relationships.

United Midwayers of Urantia, joint corps of the loyal primary and secondary midwayers, formed after Pentecost.

Universal Absolute, coordinator and unifier of Qualified (Deity) and Unqualified Absolutes.

Universal Father, First Source and Center, the absolute of personality.

Universal Censors, Stationary Sons of the Trinity; the judgment of the Paradise Trinity in the grand universe.

Universal Conciliators, Messenger Hosts of Space; traveling courts of the worlds, devoted to the quick adjudication of minor difficulties.

Universe Aids, generic name of unrevealed and the seven revealed orders of the local universe personalities; perform various functions in local universes.

Universe Circuit Supervisors, Higher Personalities of the Infinite Spirit, exclusive creation of the Infinite Spirit; direct and manipulate all higher spirit-energy circuits outside the Isle of Paradise.

Universe, 1. *see* **local universe**.

    2. *see* master universe.

Universe Circuit Supervisors, creation of the Infinite Spirit; direct and manipulate spirit-energy circuits outside the Isle of Paradise.

Universe Orientators, third group of the supreme seraphim; prepare ascending pilgrims for a new level of achievement.

Universe power, energy of gravity control.

Universe Power Directors, generic name of the several orders of beings having to do with the intelligent regulation of energy throughout the grand universe.

Universe reflectivity, unique phenomenon, which allows to see, hear, and feel everything in the superuniverse by means of coordinating all levels of universe reality.

Universe Sons, *see* **Creator Sons**.

Universe Spirits, *see* **Creative Spirits**.

Univitatia, offspring of the Creator Son and Creative Spirit; permanent citizens of Edentia and its associated worlds.

Unnamed Reflectivator Liaisons of Majeston, unrevealed order.

Unpervaded space, vertical space, devoid of forces, energies, and presences.

Unqualified Absolute, absolute entity, devoid of personality, divinity, and creator prerogatives; the energy potential of infinite cosmos.

Unqualified Supervisors of the Supreme, personalization of time-space supremacy; function as advisers and counselors in advanced evolutionary units of creation.

Ur, city, later city-state in southern Mesopotamia (Sumer).

Ural Mountains, mountain range in west-central Russia.

Ural Straits, ancient strait connecting the arctic seas with the Mediterranean.

Urantia, inhabited world number 606 of Satania in the local universe of Nebadon; the local universe name of our planet.

Uriah, [Uriah the Hittite] killed by order of David who then married his wife, Bathsheba.

Urmia, [*also* Orumiyeh, Urumiyeh]   1.   Lake in NW Iran.
2.   Ancient Persian town.

Ur of Chaldea, city in ancient Chaldea, land in S Babylonia.

Usatia, chief of the Census Directors of Orvonton.

Uversa, headquarters of the superuniverse of Orvonton.

Uzziah, *see* **Azariah**.

V

Van,   1.   Member of the corporeal staff; director of the supreme court of tribal coordination and racial cooperation; leader of the loyal members of the corporeal stuff of Prince Caligastia and midwayers; member of the advisory council associated with the Melchizedek receivers.
2.   Lake in Asia Minor, named after Van.

Vanished Adjusters, fourth, and unknown, stage of service of Thought Adjusters.

Vanites, mixed race of Nodites and Amadonites.

Vedism, religion of the ancient Indo-European-speaking peoples; takes its name from the collections of sacred texts known as the Vedas.

Ventriloquism

Ventriloquism, production of the voice in such a way that the sound seems to come from a source other than the vocal organs of the speaker.

Venus,   1.   Ancient Italian goddess of cultivated fields and gardens, later identified by the Romans with the Greek goddess of love, Aphrodite.

2.   Second major planet from the Sun.

Vergil, [*also* Virgil, Publius Vergilius Maro, 70-19 BC] Roman poet.

Veronica, woman from Caesarea-Philippi healed by Jesus.

Vertebrates, chordates that possess a spinal column including the mammals, birds, reptiles, amphibians, and fishes.

Vesta, in Roman religion, goddess of the hearth, identified with the Greek Hestia.

Vestal virgins, in Roman religion, the six priestesses, representing the daughters of the royal house, who tended the state cult of Vesta.

Vestment, garment worn by a priest or ecclesiastic; a priestly robe.

Vicegerington, one of the Paradise satellites; sacred world of the Father, the "bosom of the Father and the Son"; contains the secrets of trinitization.

Vilton, tertiary Lanonandek; system recorder of Satania.

Violet race, offspring of Planetary Adam and Eve; the ninth human race of Urantia.

Virgin Adjusters, Adjusters serving on their initial assignment in the minds of evolutionary candidates for eternal survival.

Vishnu, one of the principal Hindu deities, worshipped as the protector and preserver of the world and restorer of dharma (moral order).

Voices of Mercy, second group of the superior seraphim; mercy ministers of the local universes; foster the higher impulses and holier emotions of men and angels.

Voices of the Angelic Hosts, primary seconaphim; reflect sentiments of all orders of angels to the Ancients of Days.

Voices of the Conjoint Actor, primary seconaphim; interpret the mind of the Infinite Spirit to the Ancients of Days.

Voices of the Creator Sons, primary seconaphim; reflect the minds of the Creator Sons to the Ancients of Days.

Voices of the Garden, first group of the planetary helpers; personal seraphim of Material Sons and Daughters.

Voices of the Seven Master Spirits, primary seconaphim; personal representatives of the Seven Master Spirits before the Ancients of Days.

Voices of Wisdom, secondary seconaphim; living focalizations of the coordinated wisdom of the universe of universes.

Volga, river of Europe, the longest of the continent.

Volvox, flagellated unicellular green algae that form spherical colonies.

Vorondadeks, local universe Sons; perform legislative functions indigenous to the constellation governments and, as Most Highs, serve as rulers of constellations.

Vosges, massif in NE France.

W

Wales, component country of the United Kingdom.

Wampum, tubular shell beads assembled into strings or woven into belts or embroidered ornaments, formerly used as a medium of exchange by some N American Indians.

Waters of Merom, perennial spring in Upper Galilee, NW of Zefat.

Watch, [hist.] period in the night.

Western Ghats, mountain range in India.

West Indies, crescent-shaped group of islands separating the Gulf of Mexico and the Caribbean Sea from the Atlantic Ocean.

Will creature, intelligent being, possessing will.

Wisdom of Solomon, apocryphal work [noncanonical for Jews and Protestants] but included in the Septuagint [Greek translation of the Old Testament].

Witch of Endor, female sorcerer visited by King Saul who asked her to conjure up the spirit of the prophet Samuel to tell his fortunes.

Wolvering, a local universe in Orvonton.

World of the Father, seventh transitional culture world.

World of the Sons, fifth transitional culture world.

World of the Spirit, sixth transitional culture world.

X

Xenophanes, [?560-?478 BC] Greek poet and rhapsode, religious thinker, and reputed precursor of the Eleatic school of philosophy.

Y

Yahweh, god of the southern Palestinian tribes, later god of all Israel.

Yang, masculine active principle in nature that in Chinese cosmology is exhibited in light, heat, or dryness and that combines with yin to produce all that comes to be.

Yangtze, river in E Asia.

Yellow race, one of the three primary evolutionary races of Urntia.

Yellow river, river in East Asia.

Yin, feminine passive principle in nature that in Chinese cosmology is exhibited in darkness, cold, or wetness and that combines with yang to produce all that comes to be.

Z

Zaccheus, chief tax collector of Jericho.

Zacharias, father of John the Baptist.

Zaphon, one of the Decapolis cities.

Zebedee, boatbuilder from Capernaum, father of Apostles John and James.

Zebulun

Zebulun, ancient town in Galilee.

Zeus, in ancient Greek religion, chief deity of the pantheon, a sky and weather god identical with the Roman god Jupiter.

Zophar, comforter of Job.

Zoroaster, [c. 628-c. 551 BC] Iranian religious reformer and founder of Zoroastrianism.

Zoroastrianism, [Parsiism] Persian religion founded in the 6th century BC by Zoroaster and characterized by worship of a supreme god Ahura Mazda who requires good deeds for help in his cosmic struggle against the evil spirit Ahriman.

Zulu, nation in KwaZulu/Natal province, S Africa.93

DEFINITIONS

quoted from The Urantia Book

A

Ability, *[p.1779]* **Ability** is that which you inherit, while skill is what you acquire. Life is not real to one who cannot do some one thing well, expertly. Skill is one of the real sources of the satisfaction of living. **Ability** implies the gift of foresight, farseeing vision.

[p. 1876] **Ability** is the practical measure of life's opportunities. You will never be held responsible for the accomplishment of that which is beyond your **abilities**.

Absoluta, *[p. 469]* Space potency is a prereality: it is the domain of the Unqualified Absolute and is responsive only to the personal grasp of the Universal Father, notwithstanding that it is seemingly modifiable by the presence of the Primary Master Force Organizers. On Uversa, space potency is spoken of as **ABSOLUTA**. *(Also see 126)*

Absolute Level, *(p.2)* The **absolute level** is beginningless, endless, timeless, and spaceless. For example: On Paradise, time and space are nonexistent; the time-space status of Paradise is absolute. This level Is Trinity attained, existentially. by the Paradise Deities, but, this third level of unifying Deity expression is not fully unified experientially. Whenever, wherever, and however the **absolute level** of Deity functions, Paradise-absolute values and meanings are manifest.

Absolutum, *[p.120]* The eternal Isle is composed of a single form of materialization—stationary systems of reality. This literal substance of Paradise is a homogeneous organization of space potency not to be found elsewhere in all the wide universe of universes. It has received many names in different universes, and the Melchizedeks of Nebadon long since named it **absolutum**. This Paradise source material is neither dead nor alive: it is the original nonspiritual expression of the First Source and Center; it is Paradise, and Paradise is without duplicate.

Abstraction, *[p. 42]* Philosophers commit their gravest error when they are misled into the fallacy of abstraction, the practice of focusing the attention upon one aspect of reality and then of pronouncing such an isolated aspect to be the whole truth.

Actual, *[p. 1262]* From the time viewpoint, the **Actual** is that which was and is: the Potential is that which is becoming and will be: the Original is that which is. From the eternity viewpoint, the differences between the Original, the **Actual**, and the Potential are not thus apparent. These triune qualities are not so distinguished on Paradise-eternity levels. In eternity all is—only has all not yet been revealed in time and space. From a creature's viewpoint, actuality is substance, potentiality is capacity. **Actuality** exists centermost and expands therefrom into peripheral infinity.

Adventure, supreme *[p. 1729]* And for a long time there will live on earth those timid, fearful, and hesitant Individuals who will prefer thus to secure their religious consolations, even though, in so casting their lot with the religions of authority, they compromise the sóvereignty of personality, debase the dignity of self—respect, and utterly surrender the right to participate in that most thrilling and inspiring of all possible human experiences: the personal quest for truth, the exhilaration of facing the perils of intellectual discovery, the determination to explore the realities of personal religious experience, the **supreme** satisfaction of experiencing the personal triumph of the actual realization of the victory of spiritual faith over intellectual doubt as it is honestly won in the **supreme adventure** of all human existence—man seeking God, for himself and as himself, and finding him.

Affectation, *[p. 557]* **Affectation** is the ridiculous effort of the ignorant to appear wise, the attempt of the barren soul to appear rich.

Agondonters, [p. 579] On Jerusem the ascenders from these Isolated worlds occupy a residential sector by themselves and are known as the *agondonters*, meaning evolutionary will creatures who can believe without seeing, persevere when isolated, and triumph over insuperable difficulties even when alone.

Altruism, *[p. 51]* Service of one's fellows.

Ambition, *[p. 557]* **Ambition** is dangerous until it is fully socialized. You have not truly acquired any virtue until your acts make you worthy of it.

Angelic Hosts, *[p. 1841]* The **angelic hosts** are a separate order of created beings; they are entirely different from the material order of mortal creatures, and they function as a distinct group of universe intelligences. Angels are not of that group of creatures called the "Sons of God" in the Scriptures: neither are they the glorified spirits of mortal men who have gone on to progress through the mansions on high. Angels are a direct creation, and they do not reproduce themselves. The **angelic hosts** have only a spiritual kinshio with the human race. As man progresses in the journey to the Father in Paradise, he does traverse a state of being at one time analogous to the state of the angels, but mortal man never becomes an angel.

The Angels never die as man does. The angels are immortal unless, perchance, they become involved in sin as did some of them with the deceptions of Lucifer. The angels are the spirit servents in heaven, and they are neither all-wise nor all-powerful. But all of the loyal angels are truly pure and holy.

Anger, *[p. 1673]* **Anger** is a material manifestation which represents, in a general way, the measure of the failure of the spiritual nature to gain control of the combined intellectual and physical natures. **Anger** indicates your lack of tolerant brotherly love plus your lack of self—respect and self—control. **Anger** depletes the health, debases the mind, and handicaps the spirit teacher of man's soul. Have you not read in the Scriptures that "wrath kills the foolish man," and that man "tears himself in his **anger**"? That "he who is slow of wrath is of great understanding," while "he who is hasty of temper exalts folly"? You all know that "a soft answer turns away wrath," and how "grievous words stir up **anger**." Discretion defers **anger**, while "he who has no control over his own self is like a defenseless city without walls." "Wrath is cruel and anger is outrageous." "Angry men stir up strife, while the furious multiply their transgressions." "Be not hasty in spirit, for **anger** rests in the bosom of fools."

Apostle, *[p. 1525]* From this day on the term **apostle** was employed to distinguish the chosen family of Jesus' advisers from the vast multitude of believing disciples who subsequently followed him.

Appreciation, aesthetic, *[p.646]* Love of the beautiful and ever-advancing appreciation of the artistic touch of all creative manifestations on all levels of reality.

Art, *[p.2096]* **Art** results from man's attempt to escape from the lack of beauty in his material environment; it is a gesture toward the morontia level.

Atheism, *[p.646]* Hence materialism, **atheism**, is the maximation of ugliness, the climax of the finite antithesis of the beautiful

Atonement, *[p. 2017]* When once you grasp the idea of God as a true and loving Father, the only concept which Jesus ever taught, you must forthwith, in all consistency, utterly abandon all those primitive notions about God as an offended monarch, a stern and all-powerful ruler whose chief delight is to detect his subjects in wrongdoing and to see that they are adequately punished, unless some being almost equal to himself should volunteer to suffer for them, to die as a substitute and in their stead. The whole idea of ransom and **atonement** is incompatible with the concept of God as it was taught and exemplified by Jesus of Nazareth. The infinite love of God is not secondary to anything in the divine nature. All this concept of **atonement** and sacrificial salvation is rooted and grounded in selfishness.

This entire idea of the ransom of the **atonement** places salvation upon a plane of unreality; such a concept is purely philosophic.

B

Baal, *[p.1064]* The northern and more settled Canaanltes (the Baalites) freely bought, sold, and mortgaged their lands. The word **Baal** means owner. The **Baal** cult was founded on two major doctrines: First, the validation of property exchange, contracts, and covenents—the right to buy and sell land. Second, **Baal** was supposed to send rain—he was a god of fertility of the soil. Good crops depended on the favor of **Baal**. The cult was largely concerned with *land*, its ownership and fertility. In general the Baalites owned houses,lands, and slaves. They were the aristocratic landlords and lived in the cities. Each **Baal** had a sacred place, a priesthood, and the "holy women," the ritual prostitutes.

Baptism of the Spirit, *[p.2061]* The term "**baptism of the spirit**," which came into such general use about this time, merely signified the conscious reception of this gift of the Spirit of Truth and the personal acknowledgment of this new spiritual power as an augmentation of all spiritual influences previously experienced by God—knowing souls.

Beauty, *[p. 43]* Truth,**beauty**,and goodness are divine realities, and as man ascends the scale of spiritual living, these supreme qualities of the Eternal become increasingly co-ordinated and unified in God, who is love.

[p. 646] Philosophy you somewhat grasp, and divinity you comprehend in worship, social service, and personal spiritual experience, but the pursuit of **beauty**—cosmology—you all too often limit to the study of man's crude artistic endeavors. **Beauty**, art, is largely a matter of the unification of contrasts. Variety is essential to the concept of **beauty**. The supreme **beauty**, the height of finite art, is the drama of the unification of the vastness of the cosmic extremes of Creator and creature. Man finding God and God finding man— the creature becoming perfect as is the Creator—that is the supernal achievement of the supremely beautiful, the attainment of the apex of cosmic art.

[p. 647] **Beauty** is the intellectual recognition of the harmonious time-space synthesis of the far-flung diversification of phenomenal reality, all of which stems from pre-existent and eternal oneness.

Belief, *[p. 1114]* **Belief** has attained the level of faith when it motivates life and shapes the mode of living. The acceptance of a teaching as true is not faith; that is mere **belief**. Neither is certainty nor conviction faith. A state of mind attains to faith levels only when it actually dominates the mode of living. Faith is a living attribute of genuine personal religious experience. One believes truth, admires beauty, and reverences goodness, but does not worship them; such an attitude of saving faith is centered on God alone, who is all of these personified and infinitely more.

Belief is always limiting and binding; faith is expanding and releasing. **Belief** fixates, faith liberates.But living religious faith is more than the association of noble **beliefs**; it is more then an exalted system of philosophy; it is a living experience concerned with spiritual meanings, divine ideals, and supreme values; it is God—knowing and man-serving.

[p. 1114] **Beliefs** may become group possessions, but faith must be personal. Theologic **beliefs** can be suggested to a group, but faith can rise up only in the heart of the individual religionist.

Birth, New, *[p. 1545]* Jesus made plain to his apostles the difference between the repentance of so-called good works as taught by the Jews and the change of mind by faith— the **new birth**—which he required as the price of admission to the kingdom.

[p.1660] Men are, indeed, by nature evil, but not necessarily sinful. The **new birth**—the baptism of the spirit—is essential to deliverance from evil and necessary for the entrance into the kingdom of heaven.

Body, Human, *[p. 8]* *Body*. The material or physical organism of man. The living electrochemical mechanism of animal nature and origin.

[p. 1216] Material evolution has provided you a life machine, your body;

[p. 141] In time, man's body is just as real as mind or spirit, but in death, both mind (identity) arid spirit survive while the body does not.

Bravery, [p. 1608] The courage of the flesh is the lowest form of **bravery**. Mind **bravery** is a higher type of human courage but the highest and supreme is uncompromising loyalty to the enlightened convictions of profound spiritual realities. And such courage constitutes the heroism of the God-knowing man.

C

Causation, *[p. 192]* The reality domain of the physical senses, the scientific realms of logical uniformity, the differentiation of the factual and the nonfactual, reflective conclusions based on cosmic response. This is the mathmatical form of the cosmic discrimination

Chance, *[p. 951]* **Chance** is a word which signifies that man is too ignorant or too indolent to determine causes. Men regard a natural occurrence as an accident or as bad luck only when they are destitute of curiosity and imagination, when the reces lack initiative and adventure. Exploration of the phenomena of life sooner or later destroys man's belief in **chance**, luck, and so called accidents, substituting therefor a universe of law and order wherein all effects are preceded by definite causes. This is the fear of existence replaced by the joy of living.

Christianity, *[p. 2059]* **Christianity**, as it developed from that day, is: the fact of God as the Father of the Lord Jesus Christ, in association with the experience of believer-fellowship with the risen and glorified Christ.

Circles, psychic, *[p. 1211]* Perhaps these **psychic circles** of mortal progression would be better denominated *cosmic levels* actual meaning grasps and value realizations of progressive approach to the morontia consciousness of initial relationship of the evolutionary soul with the emerging Supreme Being. And it is this very realtionship that makes it forever impossible fully to explain the significance of the cosmic circles to the material mind. These circle attainments are only relatively related to God-consciousness. A seventh or sixth circler can be almost as truly God-knowing— sonship conscious— as a second or first circler, but such lower circle beings are far less conscious of experiential relation to the Supreme Being, universe citizenship. The attainment of these cosmic circles will become a part of the ascenders experience on the mansion worlds if they fail of such acheivement before natural death.

Conduct, *[p. 301]* Proper **conduct** is essential to progress by way of knowledge, through philosophy, to the spiritual heights of spontaneous worship. All Paradise **conduct** is wholly spontaneous, in every sense natural and free. But there still is a proper and perfect way of doing things on the eternal Isle, and the directors of **conduct** are ever by the side of the "strangers within the gates" to instruct them and so guide their steps as to put them at perfect ease and at the same time to enable the pilgrims to avoid that confusion and uncertainty which would otherwise be inevitable. Only by such arrangement could endless confusion be avoided; and confusion never appears on Paradise.

Confession, *[p. 984]* The **confession** of sin is a manful repudiation of disloyalty, but it in no wise mitigates the time-space consequences of such disloyalty. But **confession**—sincere recognition of the nature of sin— is essential to religious growth and spiritual progress.

Conflict, *[p. 1221]* All **conflict** is evil in that it inhibits the creative finction of the inner life—it is a species of civil war in the personality.

Conjoint Actor, *[p. 96]* Ever remember that the Infinite Spirit is the ***Conjoint Actor***; both the Father and the Son are functioning in and through him; he is present not only as himself but also as the Father and as the Son and as the Father-Son. In recognition of this and for many additional reasons the spirit presence of the Infinite Spirit is often referred to as "the spirit of God."

[p. 8] The **Conjoint Actor** is the spirit-mind personality, the source of intelligence, reason, and the universal mind.

Conscience, *[p. 1005]* **Conscience**, untaught by experience and unaided by reason, never has been, and never can be a safe and unerring guide to human conduct. **Conscience** is not a divine voice speaking to the human soul. It is merely the sum total of the moral and ethical content of the mores of any current stage of existence; It simply represents the humanly conceived ideal of reaction in any given set of circumstances.

Constellation, *[p. 166]* One hundred systems (about 100,000 inhabitable planets) make up a **constellation**. Each **constellation** has an architectural headquarters sphere and is presided over by three Vorondadek Sons, the Most High. Each **constellation** also has a Faithful of Days in observation, an ambassador of the Paradise Trinity.

Cosmic Consciousness, *[p. 3]* **Cosmic consciousness** implies the recognition of a First Cause, the one and only uncaused reality.

Counsel, *[p. 402]* The social urge, the endowment of species co-operation; the ability of will creatures to harmonize with their fellows; the origin of the gregarious instinct among the more lowly creatures.

Courage, *[p. 402]* The fidelity endowment—in personal beings, the basis of character acquirement and the intellectual root of moral stamina and spiritual bravery. When enlightened by facts and inspired by truth, this becomes the secret of the urge of evolutionary ascension by the channels of intelligent and conscientious self—direction.

[p. 51] ***Courage***—strength of character.

[p. 1223] **Courage** is valorous,

[p. 1641] **Courage** is the confidence of thoroughgoing honesty about those things which one professes to believe. Sincere men are unafraid of the critical examination of their true convictions and noble ideals.

Cult, *[p. 966]* A symbolism of rituals, slogans, or goals. The **cult** is the skeletal structure around which grows the living and dynamic body of personal spiritual experience—true religion.

Curiosity, *[p. 646]* Hunger for harmony and thirst for beauty. Persistent attempts to discover new levels of harmonious cosmic relationships.

D

Day, *[p. 519]* The Satania **day** equals three **days** of Urantia time, less one hour, four minutes, and fifteen seconds, that being the time of the axial revolution of Jerusem.

[p. 372] The **day** in Satania, as reckoned on Jerusem, is a little less (1 hour,4 minutes, 15 seconds) than three **days** of Urantia time. These times are generally known as Salvington time, and Satania or system time. Standard time is universe time. The standard **day** of Nebadon is equal to eighteen **days** and six hours of Urantia time, plus two and one-half minutes.

Death, [p. 540] Mortal **death** is a technique of escape from the material life in the flesh.

[p. 1229] Urantians generally recognize only one kind of **death**, the physical cessation of life energies; but concerning personality survival there are really three kinds:

1. *Spiritual (soul)* **death.** If and when mortal man has finally rejected survival, when he has been pronounced spiritually insolvent, morontially bankrupt, in the conjoint opinion of the Adjuster and the surviving seraphim, when such co-ordinate advice has been recorded on Uversa, and after the Censors and their reflective associates have verified these findings, thereupon do the rulers of Orvonton order the immediate release of the indwelling Monitor. But this release of the Adjuster in no way affects the duties of the personal or group seraphim concerned with that Adjuster-abandoned individual. This kind of **death** is final in its significance irrespective of the temporary continuation of the living energies of the physical and mind mechanisms. From the cosmic standpoint the mortal is already dead; the continuing life merely indicates the persistence of the material momentum of cosmic energies.

2. *Intellectual (mind)* **death.** When the vital circuits of higher adjutant ministry are disrupted through the aberrations of intellect or because of the partial destruction of the mechanism of the brain, and if these conditions pass a certain critical point of irreparability, the indwelling Adjuster is immediately released to depart for Divinington. On the universe records a mortal personality is considered to have met with death whenever the essential mind circuits of human will-action have been destroyed. And again, this is **death**, irrespective of the continuing function of the living mechanism of the physical body. The body minus the volitional mind is no longer human, but according to the prior choosing of the human will, the soul of such an individual may survive.

3. *Physical (body and mind)* **death.** When **death** overtakes a human being, the Adjuster remains in the citadel of the mind until it ceases to function as an intelligent mechanism, about the time that the measurable brain energies cease their rhythmic vital pulsations. Following this dissolution the Adjuster takes leave of the vanishing mind, just as unceremoniously as entry was made years before, and proceeds to Divinington by way of Uversa.

[p. 1230] After **death** the material body returns to the elemental world from which it was derived, but two nonmaterial factors of surviving personality persists: The pre-existent Thought Adjuster, with the memory transcription of the mortal career, proceeds to Divinington; and there also remains, in the custody of the destiny guardian, the immortal morontial soul of the deceased human. These phases and forms of soul, these once kenetic but now static formulas of identity, are essential to repersonalization on the morontia worlds; and it the reunion of the Adjuster and the soul that reassembles the surviving personality, that reconsciousizes you at the time of the morontia awakening.

Defeat

For those who do not have personal seraphic guardians, the group custodians faithfully and effeciently perform the same service of identity safekeeping and personality resurrection. The seraphim him are indispensible to the reassembly of personality.

Upon **death** the Thought Adjuster temporarily loses personality, but not identity; the human subject temporarily loses identity, but not personality; on the mansion worlds both reunite in eternal manifectation. Never does a departed Thought Adjuster return to earth as the being of former indwelling; never is personality manifested without the human will; and never does a dis-Adjustered human being after **death** manifest active identity or in any manner establish communication with the living beings of earth. Such dis-Adjustered souls are wholly and absolutely unconscious during the long or short sleep of death. There can be no exhibition of any sort of personality or ability to engage in communications with other personalities until after completion of survival. Those who go to the mansion worlds are not permitted to send messages back to their loved ones. It is the policy throughout the universes to forbid such communication during the period of a current dispensation.

[p. 1231] When **death** of a material, intellectual, or spiritual nature occurs, the Adjuster bids farewell to the mortal host and departs for Divinington.

[p. 2016] **Death** is, ordinarily, a part of life. **Death** is the last act in the mortal drama.

Defeat, *[p. 1740]* **Defeat** is the true mirror in which you may honestly view your real self.

Deity, *[p. 2]* **Deity** is personalizable as God, is prepersonal and superpersonal in ways not altogether comprehensible by man. **Deity** is characterized by the quality of unity—actual of potential—on all supermaterial levels of reality; and this unifying quality is best comprehended by creatures as divinity.

[p. 3] **Deity** is the source of all that which is divine. **Deity** is characteristically and invariably divine, but all that which is divine is not necessarily **Deity**, though it will be co-ordinated with **Deity** and will tend towards some phase of unity with **Deity**—spiritual, mindal, or personal.

Democracy, *[p. 970]* Men have also made a fetish of **democracy**, the exultation and adoration of the common man's ideas when collectively called "public opinion." One man's opinion, when taken by itself is not regarded as worth much, but when many men are collectively functioning as a **democracy**, this same mediocre judgement is held to be the arbiter of justice and the standard of righteousness.

Destiny, spiritual, *[p. 1739]* **Spiritual destiny** is dependent on faith, love,and devotion to truth—hunger and thirst for righteousness—the wholehearted desire to find God and to be like him.

Devil, *[p. 602]* The "**devil**" is none other than Caligastia, the deposed Planetary Prince of Urantia and a Son of the secondary order of Lanonandeks. At the time Michael was on Urantia in the flesh, Lucifer, Satan, and Caligastia were leagued together to effect the miscarriage of his bestowel mission. But they signally failed.

Divinity, *[p. 3]* **Divinity** is the characteristic, unifying, and co-ordinating quality of Deity. **Divinity** is creature comprehensible as truth, beauty, and goodness; correlated in personality as love, mercy, and ministry; disclosed on impersonal levels as Justice, power, and sovereighty.

Divinity may be perfect—complete—as on existential and creator levels of Paradise perfection; it may be imperfect, as on experiential and creature levels of time—space evolution; or it may be relative, neither perfect not imperfect, as on certain Havona levels of existential-experiential relationships.

Divorce, *[p. 929]* It is also unfortunate that certain groups of mortals have conceived of marriage as being consummated by divine action. Such beliefs lead directly to the concept of the indissolubility of the marital state regardless of the circumstances or the wishes of the contracting parties. But the very fact of marriage dissolution itself indicates that Deity is not a conjoining party to such unions. If God has once joined any two things or persons together, they will remain thus joined until such a time as the divine will decrees their separation. But, regarding marriage, which is a human institution, who shall presume to sit in judgement, to say which marriages are unions that might be approved by the universe supervisors in contrast with those which are purely human in nature and origin?

Doctrine, *[p. 969]* In olden times the fetish word of authority was a fear-inspiring *doctrine*, the most terrible of all tyrants which enslave men. A doctrinal fetish will lead mortal man to betray himself into the clutches of bigotry, fanaticism, superstition, intolerance, and the most atrocious of barbarous cruelties. Modern respect for wisdom and truth is but the recent escape from the fetish—making tendency up to the higher levels of thinking and reasoning. Concerning the accumulated fetish writings which various religionists hold as *sacred books*, it is not only believed that what is in the book is true, but also that *every* truth is contained in the book. If one of these sacred books happens to speak of the earth as being flat, then, for long generations, otherwise sane men and women will refuse to accept positive evidence that the planet is round.

Dogmatism, *[p. 1092]* Sectarianism is a disease of institutuinal religion, and **dogmatism** is an enslavement of the spiritual nature. It is far better to have a religion without a church than a church without religion.

Duty, *[p. 192]* [as a level of reality] The reality domain of morals in the philosophic realm, the arena of reason, the recognition of relative right and wrong. This is the judicial form of the cosmic discrimination.

E

Egotism, *[p. 1223]* Of all the dangers which beset man's mortal nature and jeopardize his spiritual integrity, pride is the greatest. Courage is valorous, but **egotism** is vainglorious and suicidal. Reasonable self—confidence is not to be deplored. Man' ability to transcend himself is the one thing which distinguishes him from the animal kingdom.

El

El, *[p. 1053]* Amid all this confusion of terminology and haziness of concept, many devout believers sincerely endeavored to worship all of these evolving ideas of divinity, and there grew up the practice of referring to this composite Deity as **El**. And this term included still other of the Bedouin nature gods.

El Elyon, *[p. 1053]* For centuries after Melchizedek's sojourn at Salem his doctrine of Deity persisted in various versions but was generally connoted by the term **El Elyon**, the Most High God of heaven.

El Shaddai, *[p. 1053]* This idea of God was a composite derived from the teachings of Amenamope's Book of Wisdom modified by Ikhnaton's doctrine of Aton and further influenced by Melchizedek's teachings embodied in the concept of El Elyon. But as the concept of **El Shaddai** permeated the Hebrew mind, it became thoroughly colored with the Yahweh beliefs of the desert. One of the dominant ideas of the religion of this era was the Egyptian concept of divine Providence, the teaching that material prosperity was a reward for serving **El Shaddai**.

Elohim, *[p. 1053]* In Kish and Ur there long persisted Sumerian-Chaldean groups who taught a three-in-one God concept founded on the traditions of the days of Adam and Melchizedek. This doctrine was carried to Egypt, where this Trinity was worshiped under the name of **Elohim**, or in the singular as **Eloah**.

End, *[p. 1263]* From a practical viewpoint the philosophers of the universe have come to the conclusion that there is no such thing as an *end*.

Energy, *[p. 102]* Spirit is divine purpose, and spirit mind is divine purpose in action. **Energy** is thing, mind is meaning, spirit is value.

[p. 9] **Energy** we use as an all-inclusive term applied to spiritual, mindal, and material realms.

[p. 469] In this paper, for example, the word *energy* is used to denote all phases and forms of phenomenal motion, action, and potential, while *force* is applied to the pregravity, and *power* to the post gravity, stages of **energy**.

[p. 468] **Energy** proceeds from Paradise, fashioned after the divine order. Energy—pure **energy**—partakes of the nature of the divine organization; it is fashioned after the similitude of the three Gods embraced in one, as they function at the headquarters of the universe of universes.

Energy, emergent, *[p. 9]* **Emergent energy** embraces all energies which are responsive to paradise gravity but are as yet unresponsive to local or linear gravity. This is the pre—electronic level of energy—matter.

[p. 470] The passive presence of the primary force organizers is sufficient to transform space potency into primordial force, and it is upon such an activated space field that these same force organizers begin their initial and active operations. Primordial force is destined to pass through two distinct phases of transmutation in the realms of energy manifestation before appearing as universe power. These two levels of emerging energy are; *1. Puissant energy 2. Gravity energy.*

Energy, Gravity, *[p. 470]* The now appearing gravity-responding energy carries the potential of universe power and becomes the active ancestor of all universe matter. This secondary or **gravity energy** is the product of the energy elaboration resulting from the pressure-presence and the tension-trends set up by the Associate Transcendental Master Force Organizers. In response to the work of these force manipulators, space-energy rapidly passes from the puissant to the gravity stage, thus becoming directly responsive to the circular grasp of Paradise (absolute) gravity while disclosing a certain potential for sensitivity to the linear-gravity pull inherent in the soon appearing material mass of the electronic and the post-electronic stages of energy and matter.

Energy, pure, *[p. 469]* Primordial force is sometimes spoken of as *pure energy*; on Uversa we refer to it as SEGREGATA.

[p. 638] **Pure energy** is the ancestor of all relative, nonspirit functional realities, while pure spirit is the potential of the divine and directive overcontrol of all basic energy systems. And these realities, so diverse as manifested throughout space and as observed in the motions of time, are both centered in the person of the Paradise Father.

Energy, Havona, *[p. 470]* A pre-existent phase of energy which is characteristic of the central universe. Here the evolutionary cycle seems to turn back upon itself; energy——power now seems to begin to swing back towards force, but force of a nature very unlike that of space potancy and primordial force. **Havona energy** systems are not dual: they are triune. On Uversa these energies of Havona are known as TRIATA.

Energy, Physical, *[p. 9]* **Physical energy** is a term demoting all phases and forms of phenomenal motion, action, and potential.

Energy, Puissant, *[p. 470]* This is the powerful-directional, mass-movemented, mighty-tensioned, and forcible-reacting energy——gigantic energy systems set in motion by the activities of the primary force organizers. This primary or **puissant energy** is not at first definitely responsive to the Paradise-gravity pull though probably yielding an aggregate-mass or space-directional response to the collective group of absolute influences operative from the nether side of Paradise.

Energy, transcendental, *[p. 471]* This energy system operates on and from the upper level of Paradise and only in connection with the absonite peoples. On Uversa it is denominated TRANOSTA.

Error, *[p. 754]* **Error** might be regarded as a misconception or distortion of reality.

[p. 755] **Error** suggests lack of intellectual keenness; evil, deficiency of wisdom; sin, abject spiritual poverty; but iniquity is indicative of vanishing personality control.

[p. 1435] **Error** (evil) is the penalty of imperfection. **Error** is the shadow of relative incompleteness which must of necessity fall across man's ascending universe path to Paradise perfection. **Error** (evil) is not an actual universe quality; it is simply the observation of a relativity in the relatedness of the imperfection of the incomplete finite to the ascending levels of the Supreme and Ultimate.

Essenes, *[p. 1534]* The **Essenes** were a true religious sect, originating during the Maceabeean revolt, whose requirments were in some respects more exacting than those of the Pharisees. They had adopted many Persian beliefs and practices, lived as a brotherhood in monasteries, refrained from marriage, and had all things in common. They specialized in teachings about angels.

Eternity

Eternity, *[p. 364]* To me it seems more fitting, for purposes of explanation to the mortal mind, to conceive of **eternity** as a cycle and the eternal purpose as an endless circle, a cycle of **eternity** in some way synchronized with the transient material cycles of time. As regards the sectors of time connected with, and forming a part of, the cycle of **eternity**, we are forced to recognize that such temporary epochs are born, live, and die just as the temporary beings of time are born, live, and die.

The sectors of time are like the flashes of personality in temporal form; they appear for a season, and then they are lost to human sight only to reappear as new actors and continuing factors in the higher life of the endless swing around the eternal circle. Eternity can hardly be conceived as a straightaway drive, in view of our belief in a delimited universe moving over a vast, elongated circle around the central dwelling place of the Universal Father.

Frankly, **eternity** is incomprehensible to the finite mind of time. You simply cannot grasp it; you cannot comprehend it.

[p. 1295] It is helpful to man's cosmic orientation to attain all possible comprehension of Deity's relation to the cosmos. While absolute Deity is eternal in nature, the Gods are related to time as an experience in **eternity**. In the evolutionary universes **eternity** is temporal everlastingness——the everlasting *now*.

Eternal Son, *[p. 8]* The **Eternal Son** is the absolute personality, the secret of spiritual energy, morontia spirits, and perfected spirits.

[p. 73] The **Eternal Son** is the perfect and final expression of the "first" personal and absolute concept of the Universal Father. Accordingly, whenever and however the Father personally and absolutely expresses himself, he does so through his **Eternal son**, who ever has been, now is and ever will be, the living and divine Word. The **Eternal Son** is the spiritual personalization of the Paradise Father's universal and infinite concept of divine reality, unqualified spirit, and absolute personality. The **Eternal Son** is the original and only-begotten Son of God He is God the Son, the Second person of Deity and the associate creator of all things. As the Father is the First Great Source and Center, so the **Eternal Son** is the Second Great Source and Center.

[p. 74] The **Eternal Son** is the spiritual center and the divine administrator of the spiritual government of the universe of universes. The Universal Father is first a creator and then a controller; the **Eternal Son** is first a cocreator and then a *Spiritual administrator*. God is spirit, and the Son is a personal revelation of that spirit. The Eternal Son is the eternal Word of God. He is wholly like the Father; in fact, the **Eternal Son** *is* God the Father personally minifest to the universe of universes..

[p. 75] The **Eternal Son** is the great mercy minister to all creation.

Ethics, *[p. 1127]* **Ethics** is the eternal social or racial mirror which faithfully reflects the otherwise unobservable progress of internal spiritual and religious developments.

Evil, *[p. 555]* Law is life itself and not the rules of its conduct. **Evil** is a transgression of law, not a violation of the rules of conduct pertaining to life, which *is* the law.

Experience, human

[p. 754] There are many ways of looking at sin, but from the universe philosophic viewpoint sin is the attitude of a personality who is knowingly resisting cosmic reality. **Evil** is a partial realization of, or maladjustment to, universe realities. But sin is a purposeful resistance to divine reality— a conscious choosing to oppose spiritual progress— while iniquity consists in an open and persistent defiance of recognized reality and signifies such a degree of personality: disintegration as to border on cosmic insanity. [p. 755] Error suggests lack of intellectual keenness; evil, deficiency of wisdom; sin, abject spiritual poverty; but iniquity is indicative of vanishing personality control.

[p. 1220] And when creativity is turned to destructivity, you are face to face with the devastation of **evil** and sin—opression, war, and destruction. **Evil** is a partiality of creativity which tends toward disintegration and eventual destruction. All conflict is evil in that it inhibits the creative function of the inner life— it is a species of civil war in the personality.

[p. 1458] The *possibility* of **evil** is necessary to moral choosing, but not the actuality thereof. A shadow is only relatively real. Actual **evil** is not necessary as a personal experience. Potential **evil** acts equally well as a decision stimulus in the realms of moral progress on the lower levels of spiritual development. **Evil** becomes a reality of personal experience only when a moral mind makes **evil** its choice.

[p. 1660] **Evil** is the unconscious or unintended transgression of the divine law, the Father's will. **Evil** is likewise the measure of the imperfectness of obedience to the Father's will. Sin is the conscious, knowing, and deliberate transgression of the divine law, the Father's will.

Sin is the measure of unwillingness to be divinely led and spiritually directed. Iniquity is the willful, determined, and persistent transgression of the divine law, the Father's will. Iniquity is the measure of the continued rejection of the Father's loving plan of personality survival and the Sons' merciful ministry of salvation.

Evidence, [p. 114] The basis of Fairness.

Evolution, [p. 837] Progressive creation

[p. 1159] **Evolution** is creativity in time.

Evolution, spiritual, [p. 1460] **Spiritual evolution** is an experience of the increasing and voluntary choice of goodness attended by an equal and progressive diminution of the possibility of evil.

Experience, religious, [p. 1121] **Religious experience** is the realization of the consciousness of having found God. And when a human being does find God, there is experienced within the soul of that being such an indescribable restlessness of triumph in discovery that he is impelled to seek loving service-contact with his less illuminated fellows, not to disclose that he has found God, but rather to allow the overflow of the welling-up of eternal goodness within his own soul to refresh and ennoble his fellows. Real religion leads to increased social service.

Experience, human, [p. 1123] What is **human experience**? It is simply any interplay between an active and questioning self and any other active and external reality. The mass of experience is determined by depth of concept plus totality of recognition of the reality of the external. The motion of experience equals the force of expectant immagination plus the keenness of the sensory discovery of the external qualities of contacted reality. The fact of experience is found in self—consciousness plus other-existences— other-thingness, other-mindness, and other-spiritness.

Experience, Supreme, *[p. 1431]* To become acquainted with one's brothers and sisters, to know their problems and to learn to love them, is the **supreme experience** of living.

[p. 1732] The **supreme experience** of human existence; finding God for yourselves and knowing him in your own souls.

F

Failure *[p. 1780]* And it is in this business of facing **failure** and adjusting to defeat that the far-reaching vision of religion exerts its supreme influence. **Failure** is simply an educational episode——a cultural experiment in the acquirement of wisdom——in the experience of the God-seeking man who has embarked on the eternal adventure of the exploration of a universe. To such men defeat is but a new tool for the achievement of higher levels of universe reality.

The career of a God——seeking man may prove to be a great success in the light of eternity, even though the whole temporal——life enterprise may appear as an overwhelming failure, provided each life **failure** yielded the culture of wisdom and spirit achievement.

Fairness *[p. 38]* Eternal justice and divine mercy together constitute what in human experience would be called *fairness*.

[p. 114] **Fairness** (justice in harmony with mercy)

Faith, *[p. 51]* **Faith**—— the supreme assertion of human thought.

[p. 1091] Let the term "**faith**" stand for the individual's relation to God rather than for the creedal formulation of what some group of mortals have common religious attitude. "Have you **faith**? Then have it to yourself."

[p. 1105] **Faith** unites moral insight with conscientious discriminations of values, and the pre-existent evolutionary sense of duty completes the ancestry of true religion.

[p. 1106] Reason is the method of science; **faith** is the method of religion; logic is the attempted techinque of philosophy..

[p. 1108] **Faith**-insight, or spiritual intuition, is the endowment of the cosmic mind in association with the Thought Adjuster, which is the Father's gift to man.

[p. 1114] Belief has attained the level of **faith** when it motivates life and shapes the mode of living. The acceptance of a teaching as true is not **faith**; that is mere belief. Neither is certainty not conviction **faith**. A state of mind attains to **faith** levels only when it actually dominates the mode of living. **Faith** is a living attribute of genuine personal religious experience. One believes truth, admires beauty, and reverences goodness, but does not worship them; such an attitude of saving faith is centered on God alone, who is all of these personified and infinitely more. Belief is always limiting and binding; **faith** is expanding and releasing. Belief fixates, gaith liberates. But living religious **faith** is more than the association

of noble beliefs; it is more than an exalted system of philosophy; it is a living experience concerned with spiritual meanings, divine ideals, and supreme values; it is God-knowing and man-serving. Beliefs may become group possessions, but faith must be personal. Theologic beliefs can be suggested, to a group, but **faith** can rise up only in the heart of the individual religionist.

Faith has falsified its trust when it presumes to deny realities and to confer upon its devotees assumed knowledge. **Faith** is a traitor when it fosters betrayal of intellectual integrity and belittles loyalty to supreme values and divine ideals. **Faith** never shuns the problem-solving duty of mortal living. Living **faith** does not foster bigotry, persecution, or intolerance.

Faith does not shackle the creative imagination, neither does it maintain an unreasoning prejudice toward the discoveries of scientific investigation. **Faith** vitalizes religion and constrains the religionist heroically to live the golden rule. The zeal of **faith** is according to knowledge, and its strivings are the preludes to sublime peace.

[p. 1116] **Faith** becomes the connection between moral consciousness and the spiritual concept of enduring reality.

[p. 1123] Man very early becomes conscious that he is not alone in the world or the universe. There develops a natural spontaneous self-consciousness of other-mindedness in the environment of selfhood. **Faith** translates this natural experience into religion, the recognition of God as the reality—source, nature, and destiny—of *other mindedness*.

[p. 1136] **Faith** is the insight technique of religion.

[p. 1139] **Faith** is the act of recognizing the validity of spiritual consciousness—something which is incapable of other mortal proof.

[p. 1145] Through spiritual faith man gains insight into the love of God but soon discovers that this spiritual **faith** has no influence on the ordained laws of the material universe.

[p. 1459] But truth can never become man's possession without the exercise of **faith**. This is true because man's thoughts, wisdom, ethics, and ideals will never rise higher than his **faith**, his sublime hope. And all such true **faith** is predicated on profound reflection, sincere self-criticism, and uncompromising; moral consciousness. **Faith** is the inspiration of the spiritized creative imagination.

Faith acts to release the superhuman activities of the divine spark, the immortal germ, that lives within the mind of man, and which is the potential of eternal survival.

[p. 2053] "Peace be upon you. You rejoice to know that I am the resurrection and the life, but this will avail you nothing unless you are first born of the eternal spirit, thereby coming to possess, by **faith**, the gift of eternal life. If you are the faith sons of my Father, you shall never die; you shall not perish."

Faithfuls of Days, *[p. 179]* The Paradise counselors to the Most High rulers of the constellation governments.

Faithfulness, *[p. 1877]* **Faithfulness** is the unerring measure of human trustworthiness. He who is faithful in little things is also likely to exhibit **faithfulness** in everything consistent with his endowments.

Falsehood

Falsehood, *[p. 555]* **Falsehood** is not a matter of narration technique but something premeditated as a perversion of truth. The shadow of a hair's turning, premeditated for an untrue purpose, the slightest twisting or perversion of that which is principle—these constitute falseness.

Family, *[p. 941]* The **family** is the fundamental unit of fraternity in which parents and children learn those lessons of patience, altruism, tolerance, and forbearance which are so essential to the realization of brotherhood among all men.

Family life, *[p. 942]* **Family life** is the progenitor of true morality, the ancestor of the consciousness of loyalty to duty. The enforced associations of **family life** stabilize personality and stimulate its growth through the compulsion of necessitous adjustment to other and diverse personalities. But even more, a true family—a good family—reveals to the parental procreators the attitude of the Creator to his children, while at the same time such true parents portray to their children the first of a long series of ascending disclosures of the love of the Paradise parent of all universe children.

Fetishism, *[p. 967]* The concept of a spirit's entering into an inanimate object, an animal, or a human being, is a very ancient and honorable belief, having orevalled since the beginning of the evolution of religion. This doctrine of spirit possession is nothing more nor less than *fetishism*.

Finite level, *[p. 2]* The **finite level** of reality is characterized by creature life and time-space limitations. Finite realities may not have endings, but they always have beginnings— they are created. The deity level of Supremacy may be may be conceived as a function in relation to finite existences.

First Source and Center, *[p. 5]* God—the Universal Father— is the personality of the **First Source and Center**.

[p. 5] **The First Source and Center** is, therefore, primal in all domains; deified or undeified, personal or impersonal, actual or potential, finite or infinite. No thing or being, no relativity or finality, exists except in direct or indirect relation to, and dependence on, the primacy of the **First Source and Center**.

Force, *[p. 9]* Energy we use as an all-inclusive term applied to spiritual, mindal, and material, realms. *Force* is also thus broadly used.

Force, cosmic, *[p. 9]* **Cosmic force** embraces all energies deriving from the Unqualified Absolute but which are as yet unresponsive to Paradise gravity.

Force, Primordial, *[p. 469]* This represents the first basic change in space potency and may be one of the nether Paradise functions of the Unqualified Absolute. We know that the space presence going out from nether Paradise is modified in some manner from that which is incoming. But regardless of any such possible relationships, the openly recognized transmutation of space potency into primordial force is the primary differentating function of the tension-presence of the living paradise force organizers.

Passive and potential force becomes active and primordial in response to the resistance afforded by the space presence of the Primary Eventuated Master Force Organizers. Force is now emerging from the exclusive domain of the Unqualified Absolute into the realms of multiple response—response to certain primal motions initiated by the God of Action and thereupon to certain compensating motions emanating from the Universal Absolute.

Primordial force is seemingly reactive to transcendental causation in proportion to absoluteness. Primordial force is sometimes spoken of as *pure energy*: on Uversa we refer to it as SEGREGATA.

G

Goal of time, [p. 557] The finding of God on Paradise.

God, *[p. 3]* **GOD** is a word symbol designating all personalizations of Deity. The term requires a different definition on each level of Deity function and must be still further redefined within each of these levels, as this term may be used to designate the diverse co-ordinate and subordinate personalizations of Deity; for example: the Paradise Creator Sons— the local universe fathers.

The term **God,** as we make use of it, may be understood:

By designation—as **God** the Father

By context—as when used in the discussion of some one deity level or association. When in doubt as to the exact interpretation of the word **God**, it would be advisable to refer it to the person of the Universal Father..

The term **God** always denotes *personality*. Deity may, or may not refer to divinity personalities. The word **GOD** is used, in these papers, with the following meanings:

1. *God the Father*—Creator, Controller, and Upholder. The Universal Father, the First person of Deity.

2. *God the Son*—Co-ordinate Creator, Spirit Controller, and spiritual Administrator. The Eternal Son, the Second Person of Deity.

3. *God the Spirit*—Conjoint Actor, Universal Integrator, and Mind Bestower. The Infinite Spirit, the Third Person of Deity.

4. *God the Supreme*

5. *God the Sevenfold*

6. *God the Ultimate*

7. *God the Absolute*

[p. 5] **God**—the Universal Father—is the personality of the First Source and Center.

[p. 5] **God**, as the First Source and Center, is primal in relation to total reality—unqualifiedly The First Source and Center is infinite as well as eternal and is therefore limited or conditioned only by volition.

*[p. 28] **God** is personality.*

Notwithstanding that **God** is an eternal power, a majestic presence, a transcendent ideal, and a glorious spirit, though he is all these and infinitely more, nonetheless, he is truly and everlastingly a perfect Creator personality, a person who can "know and be known", who can "love and be loved," and one who can befriend us; while you can be known, as other humans have been known, as the friend of **God**. He is a real spirit and a spiritual reality.

[p. 30] **God** is to science a cause, to philosophy an idea, to religion a person, even the loving heavenly Father. **God** is to the scientist a primal force, to the philosopher a hypothesis of unity, to the religionist a living spiritual experience.

God (cont.)

[p. 5] **God** is spirit— spirit personality.

[p. 34] **God** is not a cosmic accident; neither is he a universe experimenter.

[p. 34] No thing is new to **God**, and no cosmic event ever comes as a surprise; he inhabits the circle of eternity. He is without beginning or end of days. To **God** there is no past, present, or future: all time is present at any given moment. He is the great and only I AM.

[p. 36] **God** is eternally and infinitely perfect, he cannot personally know imperfection as his own experience, but he does share the consciousness of all the experience of inperfectness of all the struggling creatures of the evolutionary universes of all the Paradies Creator Sons.

[p. 40] **God** is love, but love is not **God**.

[p. 38] **God** is inherently kind, naturally compassionate, and everlastingly merciful.

[p. 39] It is wrong to think of **God** as being coaxed into loving his children because of the sacrifices of his Sons or the intercessions of his subordinate creatures, "for the Father himself loves you." It is in reaponse to this paternal affection that **God** sends the marvelous Adjusters to indwell the minds of men. **God**'s love is universal; "whosoever will may come." He would "have all men be saved by coming into the knowledge of the truth." He is "not willing that any should perish."

[p. 41] **God** is never wrathful, vengeful, or angry. It is true that wisdom does often restrain his love, while justice conditions hes rejected mercy. His love of righteousness cannot help being exhibited as equal hatred for sin. The Father is not an inconsistent personality; the divine unity is perfect.

[p. 48] **God** is unlimited in power, divine in nature, final in will, infinite in attributes, eternal in wisdom, and absolute in reality.

[p. 55] If **God** should retire as the present upholder of all creation, there would immediately occur a universal collapse. Except for **God**, there would be no such thing as *reality*. At this very moment, as during the remote ages of the past and in the eternal future, God continues to uphold.

[p. 58] **God** repents of nothing he has ever done, now does, or ever will do. He is all-wise as well as all-powerful.

[p. 58] **God** is the only stationary, self-contained, and changeless being in the whole universe of universes, having no outside, no beyond, no past, and no future. **God** is purposive energy (creative spirit) and absolute will, and these are self-existent and universal.

Since **God** is self-existent, he is absolutely independent. The very identity of **God** is inimical to change.

[p. 59] In science, **God** is the First Causes; in religion, the universal and loving Father; in philosophy, the one being who exists by himself, not dependent on any other being for existence but beneficently conferring reality of existence on all things and upon all other beings.

[p. 60] It is an affront to **God** to believe, hold, or teach that innocent blood must be shed in order to win his favor or to divert the fictitious divine wrath.

[p. 60] What a travesty upon the infinite character of **God**! this teaching that his fatherly heart in all its austere coldness and hardness was so untouched by the

misfortunes and sorrows of his creatures that his tender mercies were not forthcoming until he saw his blameless Son bleeding and dying upon the cross of Calvary.

[p. 67] **God** is not only the determiner of destiny: he *is* man's eternal destination. All nonreligious human activities seek to bend the universe to the distorting service of self the truly religious individual seeks to identify the self with the universe and then to dedicate the activities of this unified self to the service of the universe family of fellow beings, human and superhuman.

[p. 79] God is *father personality*—the source of personality, the bestower of personality, the cause of personality.

[p. 1856] Jesus employed the word **God** to designate the *idea* of Deity and the word Father to designate the *experience* of knowing **God**. When the word Father is employed to denote **God**, it should be understood in its largest possible meaning. The word **God** cannot be defined and therefore stands for the infinite concept of the Father, while the term Father, being capable of partial definition, may be employed to represent the human concept of the divine Father as he is associated with man during the course, of mortal existence.

[p. 2095] **God** is not the mere invention of man's idealism; he is the very source of all such superanimal insights and values. **God** is not a hypothesis formulated to unify the human concepts of truth, beauty, and goodness; he is the personality of love from whom all of these universe manifestations are derived.

God-consciousness, [p. 2097] The great challenge to modern man is to achieve better communication with the divine Monitor that dwells within the human mind. Man's greatest adventure in the flesh consists in the well-balanced and sane effort to advance the borders of self-consciousness out through the dim realms of embryonic soul-consciousness in a wholehearted effort to reach the borderland of spirit-consciousness-contact with the divine presence. Such an experience constitute **God-consciousness** an experience mightily confirmative of the pre-existent truth of the religious experience of knowing God. Such spirit consciousness is the equivalent of the knowledge of the actuality of sonship with God. Otherwise, the assurance of sonship is the experience of faith. And **God-consciousness** is equivalent to the integration of the self with the universe, and on its highest levels of spiritual reality.

(24) The intellectual capacity for knowing God—**God-consciousness**.

God Seeking, *[p. 24]* The spiritual urge to find God.

God the Supreme, *[p. 11]* **God the Supreme** in Havona is the personal spirit reflection of the triune Paradise Deity.

[p. 12] The Almighty Supreme, evolving on the value-level of nonpersonal activities, and the spirit person of **God the Supreme** are *one reality*—the Supreme Being.

God the Ultimate, *[p. 12]* **God the Ultimate** Is designative of personal Deity functioning on the divinity levels of the absonite and on the universe spheres of supertime and transcended space. The Ultimate is a supersupreme eventuation of Deity. The Supreme is the Trinity unification comprehended by finite beings; the Ultimate is the unification of the Paradise Trinity comprehended by absonite beings.

Goodness

Goodness, *[p. 647]* **Goodness** embraces the sense of ethics, morality, and religion—experiential perfection-hunger.

[p. 647] **Goodness** is the mental recognition of the relative values of the diverse levels of divine perfection. The recognition of **goodness** implies a mind of moral status,a personal mind with ability to discriminate between good and evil. But the possession of **goodness**, greatness, is the measure of real divinity attainment.

[p. 1458] **Goodness** is always growing toward new levels of the increasing liberty of moral self-realization and spiritual personality attainment—the discovery of, and identification with, the indwelling Adjuster. An experience is good when it heightens the appreciation of beauty,' augments the moral will, enhances the discernment of truth, enlarges the capacity to love and serve one's fellows, exalts the spiritual ideals: and unifies the supreme human motives of time with the eternal plans of the indwelling Adjuster, all of which lead directly to an increaaed desire to do the Father's will, thereby fostering the divine passion to find God and to be more like him.

[p. 1458] **Goodness** is living, relative, always progressing, invariably a personal experience, and everlastingly correlated with the discernment of truth and beauty. **Goodness** is found in the recognition of the positive truth-values of the spiritual level, which must, in human experience, be contrasted with the negative counterpart—the shadows of potential evil.

Goodness, divine, *[p. 43]* The discernment of supreme beauty is the discovery and integration of reality: The discernment of the **divine goodness** in the eternal truth, that is ultimate beauty.

Gospel of the kingdom, *[p. 2059]* The **Gospel of the kingdom** is: the fact of the fatherhood of God, coupled with the resultant truth of the sonship-brotherhood of men.

Graciousness, *[p. 1874]* **Graciousness** is the aroma of friendliness which emanates from a love-saturated soul.

Gradent, *[p. 519]* The standard weight (of Jerusem) the **"gradent"** is built up through the decimal system from the mature ultimaton and represents almost exactly ten ounces of your weight.

Grand Universe, *[p. 129]* **The Grand Universe** is the present organized and inhabited reation. It consists of the seven superuniverses, with an aggregate evolutionary potential of around seven trillion inhabited planets, not to mention the eternal spheres of the central creation. But this tentative estimate takes no account of architectural administrative spheres, neither does it include the outlying groups of unorganized universes. The present ragged edge of the grand universe, its uneven and unfinished periphery, together with the tremendously unsettled condition of the whole astronomical plot, suggests to our star students that even the seven superuniverses are, as yet, uncompleted. As we move from within, from the divine center outward in any direction, we do, eventually, come to the outer limits of the organized and inhabited creation; we come to the outer limits of the grand universe. And it is near this outer border, in a far-off corner of such a magnificient creation, that your local universe has its eventful existence.

Growth, creative

[p. 166] ***The Grand Universe***. Seven superuniverses make up the present organized grand universe, consisting of approximately seven trillion inhabitable worlds plus the architectural spheres and the one billion inhabited spheres of Havona.

Gravita, [p. 126] The physical systems of the superuniverses are mobilized by the Universe Power Director's and their associates. These material organizations are dual in constitution and are known as **Gravita**.

[p. 470] *Universe power*. Space-force has been changed into space-energy and thence into the energy of gravity control. Thus has physical energy been ripened to that point where it can be directed into channels of power and made to serve the manifold purposes of the universe Creators. This work is carried on by the versatile directors, centers, and controller of physical energy in the grand universe——the orgainzed and inhabited creations. These Universe Power Directors assume the more or less complete control of twenty-one of the thirty phases of energy constituting the present energy system of the seven superuniverses. This domain of power-energy-matter is the realm of the intelligent activities of the Sevenfold, functioning under the time-space overcontrol of the Supreme. On Uversa we refer to the realm of universe power as **GRAVITA**.

Gravity, [p. 10] **Gravity** is the sole control of energy-matter.

[p. 125] The inescapable pull of **gravity** effectively grips all the worlds of all the universes of all space. **Gravity** is the all-powerful grasp of the physical presence of Paradise. **Gravity** is the omnipotent strand on which are strung the gleaming stars, blazing suns, and whirling spheres which constitute the universal physical adornment of the eternal God, who is all things, fills all things, and in whom all things consist.

The center and focal point of absolute material **gravity** is the Isle of Paradise, complemented by the dark **gravity** bodies encircling Havona and equilibrated by the upper and nether space reservoirs. All known emanations of nether Paradise invariable and unerringly respond to the central gravity pull operating upon the endless circuits of the elliptical space levels of the master universe. Every known form of cosmic reality has the bend of the ages, the trend of the circle, the swing of the great ellipse.

Space is nonresponsive to **gravity**, but it acts as an equilibrant on **gravity**. Without the space cushion, explosive action would jerk surrounding space bodies. Pervaded space also exerts an anti**gravity** influence upon physical or linear **gravity**; space can actually neutralize such **gravity** action even though it cannot delay it. Absolute **gravity** is paradise **gravity**. Local or linear **gravity** pertains to the electrical stage of energy or matter; it operates within the central, super-, and outer universes, wherever suitable materialization has taken place.

Growth, creative, [p. 1294] **Creative growth** is unending but ever satisfying, endless in extent but always punctuated by those personality-satisfying moments of transient goal attainment which serve so effectively as the mobilization preludes to new adventures in cosmic growth, universe exploration, and Deity attainment.

Guilt

Guilt, *[p. 1133]* The sense of **guilt** (not the consciousness of sin) comes either from interupted spiritual communion or from the lowering of one's moral ideals. Deliverance from such a predicament can only come through the realization that one's highest moral ideals are not necessarily synonymous with the will of God. Man cannot hope to live up to his highest ideals, but he can be true to his purpose of finding God and becoming more and more like him.

H

Happiness, *[p. 42]* **Happiness** ensues from the recognition of of truth because it can be *acted out*; it can be lived. Disappointment and sorrow attend upon error because, not being a reality, it cannot be realized in experience.Divine truth is best known by its *Spiritual flavor*.

    [p. 1134] Human **happiness** is achieved only when the ego desire of the self and the altruistic urge of the higher self (divine spirit) are co-ordinated and reconciled by the unified will of the integrating and supervising personality.

Harmony, *[p. 301]* **Harmony** is the keynote of the central Universe, and detectable order prevails on Paradise.

Harp of God, *[p. 539]* John the revelator saw a vision of the arrival of a class of advancing mortals from the seventh mansion world to their first heaven, the glories of Jerusem. He recorded: "And I saw as it were a sea of glass mingled with fire; and those who had gained the victory over the beast that was originally in them and over the image that persisted through the mansion worlds and finally over the last mark and trace, standing on the sea of glass, having the **harps of God**, and singing the song of deliverance from mortal fear and death." (Perfected space communication is to be had on all these worlds; and your anywhere reception of such communications is made possible by carrying the "**harp of God**," a morontia contrivance compensating for the inability to directly adjust the immature, morontia sensory mechanism to the reception of space communications.)

Hate, *[p. 1632]* **Hate** is the shadow of fear; revenge the mask of cowardice.

Havona, *[p. 129]* **Havona**, the cental universe, is not a time creation; it is an eternal existence. This never-beginning, never-ending universe consists of one billion spheres of sublime perfection and is surrounded by the enormous dark gravity bodies. At the center of Havona is the stationary and bsolutely stabilized Isle of Paradise, surrounded by its twenty-one satellites. Owing to the enormous encircling masses of the dark, gravity bodies about the fringe of the central universe, the mass content of this central creation is far in excess of the total known mass of all seven sectors of the grand universe.

Heaven, *[p. 553]* You should consider the statement about "**heaven**" and the "**heaven of heavens**." The **heaven** conceived by most of your prophets was the first of the mansion worlds of the local system. When the apostle spoke of being "caught up to the third **heaven**," he referred to that experience in which his Adjuster was detached during sleep and in this unusual state made a projection to the third of the seven mansion worlds. Some of your wise men saw the vision of the greater heaven, "the **heaven** of **heavens**," of which the sevenfold mansion world experience was but the first; the second being Jerusem; the third, Edentia and its satellites; the fourth, Salvington and the surrounding educational spheres; the fifth, Uversa; the sixth, Havona and the seventh, Paradise.

Heaven, kingdom of, *[p. 1486]* The **kingdom of heaven**, the divine government, is founded on the fact of divine sovereignty— God is spirit. Since God is spirit, this kingdom is spiritual. The **kingdom of heaven** is neither material nor merely intellectual; it is a spiritual relationship between God and man.

Holy Spirit, *[p. 95]* In your sacred writings the term *Spirit of God* seems to be used interchangeably to designate both the Infinite Spirit on Paradise and the Creative Spirit of your local universe. The **Holy Spirit** is the spiritual circuit of this Creative Daughter of the paradise Infinite Spirit. The **Holy Spirit** is a circuit indigenous to each local universe and is confined to the spiritual realm of that creation; but the Infinite Spirit is omnipresent.

[p. 190] The bestowal of the ministry spirit of a local universe Creative Spirit, known on Urantia as the **Holy Spirit**.

Home, *[p. 913]* Marriage——mating——grows out of bisexuality. Marriage is man's reactional adjustment to such bisexuality, while family life is the sum total resulting from all such evolutionary and adaptative adjustments. Marriage is enduring, it is not inherent in biologic evolution, but it is the basis of all social evolution and is therefore certain of continued existence in some form. Marriage has given mankind the **home**, and the **home** is the crowning glory of the whole long and arduous evolutionary struggle.

[p. 941] The **home** is the natural social arena wherein the ethics of blood brotherhood may be grasped by the growing children. The family is the fundamental unit of fraternity in which parents and children learn those lessons of patience, altruism, tolerance, and forbearance which are so essential to the realization of brotherhood among all men.

Hope, *[p. 51]* Is *hope*—the grandeur of trust—desirable? Then human existence must constantly be confronted with insecurities and recurrent uncertainties.

Humor, *[p. 549]* When we are tempted to magnify our self-importance, if we stop to contemplate the infinity of the greatness and grandeur of our Makers, our own self-glorification becomes sublimely ridiculous, even verging on the humerous. One of the functions of **humor** is to help all of us take ourselves less seriously. **Humor** is the divine antidote for exultation of ego.

I

I AM, *[p. 6]* The concept of the **I AM** Is a philosophic concession which we make to the time-bound, space-fettered, finite mind of man, to the impossibility of creature comprehension of eternity existences——nonbeginning, nonending realities and realtionships. To the time-space creature, all things must have a beginning save only the ONE UNCAUSED—— the primal cause of causes. Therefor do we conceptualize this philosophic value-level as the **I AM**, at the same time instructing all creatures that the Eternal Son and the Infinite Spirit are coeternal with the **I AM**; in other words, that there never was a time when the **I AM** was not the Father of the Son and, with him, of the Spirit.

Idea

Idea, *[p. 1113]* An **idea** is only a theoretical plan for action, while a positive decision is a validated plan of action.

Idealism, *[p. 51]* The approaching concept of the divine.

Image of God, *[p. 1193]* The "**image of God**" does not refer to physical likeness nor to the circumscribed limitations of material creature endowment but rather to the gift of the spirit presence of the Universal Father in the supernal bestowal of the thought adjusters upon the humble creatures of the universes.

Immaturity, *[p. 1898]* Your inability or unwillingness to forgive your fellows is the measure of your **immaturity**, your failure to attain adult sympathy, understanding, and love. *[also see maturity]*

Impatience, *[p. 557]* Impatience is a spirit poison; anger is like a stone hurled into a hornet's nest.

Iniquity, *[p. 754]* There are many ways of looking at sin, but from the universe philosophic viewpoint sin is the attitude of a personality who is knowingly resisting cosmic reality. Error might be regarded as a misconception or distortion of reality. Evil is a partial realization of, or maladjustment to, universe realities. But sin is a purposeful resistance to divine reality—a conscious choosing to oppose spiritual progress—while **iniquity** consists in an open and persistent defiance of recognized reality and signifies such a degree of personality disintegration as to border on cosmic insanity.

[p. 755] Error suggests lack of intellectual keenness; evil, deficiency of wisdom; sin, abject spiritual poverty; but **iniquity** is indicative of vanishing personality control. And when sin has so many times been chosen and so often been repeated, it may become habitual. Habitual sinners can easily become iniquitous, become wholehearted rebels against the universe and all of its divine realities. While all manner of sins may be forgiven, we doubt whether the established iniquiter would ever sincerely experience sorrow for his misdeeds or accept forgiveness for his sins.

[p. 1660] **Iniquity** is the willful, determined, and persistent transgression of the divine law, the Father's will. **Iniquity** is the measure of the continued rejection of the Father's loving plan of personality survival and the Sons' merciful ministry of salvation.

Insight,cosmic, *[p. 194]* The grasp of universe meanings.

Insight, spiritual, *[p. 1105]* All such inner and spiritual communion is termed **spiritual insight**. Such religious experiences result from the impress made upon the mind of man by the combined operations of the Adjuster and the Spirit of Truth as they function amid and upon the ideas, ideals, insights, and spirit strivings of the evolving sons of God.

[p. 1134] The mind of evolutionary man is ever confronted with the intricate problem of refereeing the contest between the natural expansion of emotional impulses and the moral growth of unselfish urges predicated on **spiritual insight**—genuine religious reflection.

Intolerance, *[p. 1641]* You should never forget that **intolerance** is the mask covering up the entertainment of secret doubts as to the trueness of one's belief. No man is at any time disturbed by his neighbor's attitude when he has perfect confidence in the truth of that which he wholeheartedly believes. Sincere men are unafraid of the critical examination of their true convictions and noble ideals.

Intuition, moral, *[p. 192]* The realization of duty.

Jehovah, *[p. 1053]* **Jehovah** is a term which in recent times has been employed to designate the completed concept of Yahweh which finally evolved in the long Hebrew experience. But the name **Jehovah** did not come into use until fifteen hundred years after the times of Jesus.

Jesus, *[p. 1426]* **Jesus** is the new and living way from man to God, from the partial to the perfect, from the earthly to the heavenly, from time to eternity.

Judgement, *[p. 114]* The final application of justice in accordance with the evidence

Justice, *[p. 114]* **Justice** is inherent in the universal sovereignty of the Paradise trinity, but goodness, mercy, and truth are the universe ministry of the divine personalities, whose Deity union constitutes the Trinity. **Justice** is not the attitude of the Father, the Son, or the Spirit. **Justice** is the Trinity attitude of these personalities of love, mercy, and ministry. No one of the paradise Deities fosters the administration of justice. **Justice** is never a personal attitude; it is always a plural function.

[p. 115] **Justice** is the collective thought of righteousness; mercy is its personal expression.

[p. 794] Natural **justice** is a man-made theory; it is not a reality. In nature, **justice** is purely theoretic, wholly a fiction. Nature provides but one kind of **justice**—inevitable conformity to causes.

Justice, as conceived by man, means getting one's rights and has, therefore, been a matter of progressive evolution. The concept of **justice** may well be constitutive in a spirit-endowed mind, but it does not spring full-fledgedly into existence on the worlds of space.

K

Keys of the kingdom, *[p. 435]* The **keys of the kingdom** of heaven are: sincerity, more sincerity , and more sincerity. All men have these keys. Men use them-advance in spirit status-by decisions, by more decisions, and by more decisions. The highest moral choice is the choice of the highest possible value, and always-in any sphere, in all of them-this is to choose to do the will of God.

Kingdom of God, *[p. 1860]* And at this time he earnestly sought to induce them to abandon the use of the term *Kingdom of God* in favor of the more practical equivalent, *the will of God*. But he did not succeed.

[p. 1860] The **kingdom of God** in this world, the supreme desire to do the will of God, the unselfish love of man which yields the good fruits of improved ethical and moral conduct.

Kingdom of Heaven, *[p. 1860]* Jesus never tired of telling them that the **knigdom of heaven** was their personal experience of realizing the higher qualities of spiritual living; that these realities of the spirit experience are pregressively translated to new and higher levels of divine certainty and eternal grandeur.

Knowledge

[p. 1088] The **kingdom of heaven** is neither a social not economic order; it is an exclusively spiritual brotherhood of God-knowing individuals.

[p. 1585] John asked Jesus, "Master, what is the **kingdom of heaven?**" and Jesus answered: "The **kingdom of heaven** consists in three essentials: first, recognition of the fact of the sovereignty of God: second, belief in the truth of sonship with God; and third, faith in the effectiveness of the supreme human desire to do the will of God-to be like God. And this is the good news of the gospel: that by faith every mortal may have all these essentials of salvation."

[p. 1727] They were commencing to comprehend that the "**kingdom of heaven** is not meat and drink but the realization of the spiritual joy of the acceptance of divine sonship."

Knowledge, *[p. 907]* **Knowledge** is power.

[p. 1120] Time is an invariable element in the attainment of **knowledge**; religion makes its endowments immediately available albeit there is the important factor of growth in grace, definite advancement in all chases of religious experience. **Knowledge** is an eternal quest; always are you learning, but never are you able to arrive at the full knowledge of absolute truth. In **knowledge** alone there can never be absolute certainty, only increasing probability of approximation; but the religious soul of spiritual illumination *knows*, and knows *now*.

[p. 1122] **Knowledge** leads to placing men, to originating social strata and castes. Religion leads to serving men, thus creating ethics and altruism. Wisdom leads to the higher and better fellowship of both ideas and one's fellows. Revelation liberates men and starts them out on the eternal adventure.

[p. 1435] **Knowledge**, is the sphere of the material or fact-discerning mind. Thuth is the domain of the spiritually endowed intellect that is conscious of knowing God. **Knowledge** is demonstrable; truth is experienced. **Knowledge** is a possession of the mind; truth an experience of the soul, the progressing self. **Knowledge** is a function of the nonspiritual level; truth is a phase of the mind-spirit level of the universes. The eye of the material mind perceives a world of factual knowledge; the eye of the spiritualized intellect discerns a world of ture values. These two views, synchronized and harmonized, reavel the world of reality, wherein wisdom interprets the phenomena of the universe in terms of progressive personal experience.

L

Law, *[p. 555]* **Law** is life itself and not the rules of its conduct. Evil is a transgression of **law**, not a violation of the rules of conduct pertaining to life, which *is* the **law**. Falsehood is not a matter of narration technique, but something premeditated as a perversion of truth.

[p. 797] **Law** is a codified record of long human experience, public opinion crystalized and legalized.

Law of the spirit, *[p. 1689]* My children, do you not perceive the **law of the spirit** which decrees that to him who has shall be given so that he shall have an abundance; but from him who has not shall be taken away even that which he has.

Levels, cosmic, *[p. 1211]* Perhaps these psychic circles of mortal progression would be better denominated *cosmic levels*— actual meaning grasps and value realizations of progressive approach to the morontia consciousness of initial relationship of the evolutionary soul with the emerging Supreme Being. And it is this very relationship that makes it forever impossible fully to explain the significance of the cosmic circles to the material mind. These circle attainments are only relatively related to God-consciousness. A seventh circler can be almost as truly God-knowing-sonship conscious-as a second or first circler, but such lower circle beings are far less conscious of experiential relation to the Supreme Being, universe citizenship. The attainment of these cosmic circles will become a part of the ascenders' experience on the mansion worlds if they fail of such achievement before natural death.

Liberty, true and false, *[p. 613]* Of all the perplexing problems growing out of the Lucifer rebellion, none has occasioned more difficulty than the failure of immature evolutionary mortals to distinguish between **true and false liberty**.

True liberty is the quest of the ages and the reward of evolutionary progress. **False liberty** is the subtle deception of the error of time and the evil of space. Enduring liberty is predicated on the reality of justice— intelligence, maturity, fraternity, and equity.

Liberty is a self-destroying technique of cosmic existence when its motivation is unintelligent, unconditioned and uncontrolled. **True liberty** is progressively related to reality and is ever regardful of social equity, cosmic fairness, universe fraternity, and divine obligations.

Liberty is suicidal when divorced from material justice, intellectual fairness, social forbearance, moral duty, and spiritual values. Liberty is nonexistent apart from cosmic reality, and all personality reality is proportional to its divinity relationships.

Unbridled self-will and unregulated self-expression equal unmitigated selfishness, the acme of ungodliness. Liberty without the associated and ever-increasing conquest of self is a figment of egoistic mortal imagination. Self motivated liberty is a conceptual illusion, a cruel deception. License madquerading in the garments of liberty is the forerunner of abject bondage.

[p. 614] **True liberty** is the associate of genuine self-respect; **false liberty** is the consort of self-admiration. **True liberty** is the fruit of self-control;**false liberty**, the assumption of self-assertion. Self control leads to altruistic services self admiration tends towards the exploitation of others for the selfish aggrandizement of such a mistaken individual as is willing to sacrifice righteous attainment for the sake of possessing unjust power over his fellow beings.

License, *[p. 613]* **License** masquerading in the garments of liberty is the forerunner of abject bondage.

Life, *[p. 404]* We speak of **life** as "energy" and as "force" but it is really neither. Force-energy is variously gravity responsive; **life** is not. Pattern is also nonresponsive to gravity, being a configuration of energies that have already fulfilled all gravity-responsive obligations. **Life**, as such, constitutes the animation of some pattern-configured or otherwise segregated system of energy-material, mindal, or spiritual.

Life (cont.)

There are some things connected with the elaboration of **life** on the evolutionary planets which are not altogether clear to us. We fully comprehend the physical organization of the electrochemical formulas of the **Life** Carriers, but we do not wholly understand the nature and source of the *life-activation spark*. We know that **life** flows from the Father through the Son and *by* the Spirit.

[p. 1124] To isolate part of **life** and call it religion is to disintegrate **life** and to distort religion And this is just why the God of worship claims all allegiance or none.

[p. 1229] The material self, the ego-entity of human identity, is dependent during the physical **life** on the continuing function of the material **life** vehicle, on the continued existence of the unbalanced equilibrium of energies and intellect which, on Urantia has been given the name *life*. But selfhood of survival value, selfhood that can transcend the experience of death, is only evolved by establishing a potential transfer of the seat of the identity of the evolving personality from the transient, **life** vehicle——the material body——to the more enduring and immortal nature of the morontia soul and on beyond to those levels whereon the soul becomes infused with, and eventually attains the status of, spirit reality. This actual transfer from material association to morontia identification is effected by the sincerity, perisistence, and steadfastness of the God-seeking decisions of the human creature.

[p. 1434] **Life** is an adaptation of the original cosmic causation to the demands and possibilities of universe situations, and it comes into being by the action of the Universal Mind and the activation of the spirit spark of the God who is spirit. The meaning of **life** is its adaptability; the value of **life** is its progressabillty—even to the heights of God consciousness

Life Carrier, *[p. 396]* Life does not originate spontaneously. Life is constructed according to plans formulated by the (unrevealed) Architects of Being and appears on the inhabited planets either by direct importation or as a result of the operations of the **Life Carriers** of the local universes. These carriers of life are among the most interesting and versatile of the diverse family of Universe sons. They are intrusted with designing and carrying creature life to the planetary spheres. And after planting this life on such new worlds, they remain, there for long periods to foster its development.

[p. 399] **Life Carriers** are living catalytic presences which agitate, organize, and vitalize the otherwise inert elements of the material order of existence.

Life, Jesus', *[p. 1393]* **Jesus' life** is the everlasting comfort of all disappointed idealists.

Light, *[p. 10]* **Light**-spirit luminosity-is a word symbol, a figure of speech, which connotes the personality manifestation characteristic of spirit beings of diverse orders. This luminous emanation is in no respect related either to intellectual insight or to physical-**light** manifestations.

Logic, *[p. 1106]* Reason is the method of science; faith is the method of religion; **logic** is the attempted technique of philosophy.

[p. 1106] Reason is the proof of science, faith the proof of religion, **logic** the proof of philosophy, but revelation is validated only by human *experience*.

[p. 1138] But **logic** can never succeed in harmonizing the findings of science and the insights of religion unless both the scientific and the religious aspects of a personality are truth dominated, sincerely desirous of following the truth wherever it may lead regardless of the conclusions which it may reach. **Logic** is the technique of philosophy, its method of expression. Within the domain of true science, reason is always amenable to genuine **logic**; within the domain of true religion, faith is always logical from the basis of an inner viewpoint, even though such faith may appear to be quite unfounded from the in-looking viewpoint of the scientific approach. From outward, looking within, the universe may appear to be material; from within, looking out, the same universe appears to be wholly spiritual. Reason grows out of material awareness, faith out of spiritual awareness, but through the mediation of a philosophy strengthened by revelation, **logic** may confirm both the inward and the outward view, thereby effecting the stabilization of both science and religion. Thus, through common contact with the **logic** of philosophy, may both science and religion become increasingly tolerant of each other, less and less skeptical.

[p. 1139] Reason, is the act of recognizing the conclusions of consciousness with regard to the experience in and with the physical world of energy and matter. Faith is the act of recognizing the validity of spiritual consciousness—something which is incapable of other mortal proof. **Logic** is the synthetic truth-seeking progression of the unity of faith and reason and is founded on the constitutive mind endowments of mortal beings, the innate recognition of things, meanings, and values.

Love, *[p. 141]* **Love** is the secret of beneficial association between personalities.

[p. 40] This term, even though it does connote man's highest concept of the mortal relations of respect and devotion, is so frequently designative of so much of human relationship that is wholly ignoble and utterly unfit to be known by any word which is also used to indicate the matchless affection of the living God for his universe creatures!

[p. 40] God is **love**, but **love** is not God. The greatest manifestation of the divine **love** for mortal beings is observed in the bestowal of the Thought Adjusters, but your greatest revelation of the Father's love is seen in the bestowal life of his Son Michael as he lived on earth the ideal spiritual life. It is the indwelling Adjuster who individualizes the love of God to each human soul.

[p. 647] Universal beauty is the recognition of the reflection of the Isle of Paradise in the material creation, while eternal truth is the special ministry of the Paradise Sons who not only bestow themselves upon the mortal races but even pour out their Spirit of Truth upon all peoples. Divine goodness is more fully shown forth in the loving ministry of the manifold personalities of the infinite Spirit. But **love**, the sum total of these three qualities, is man's perception of God as his spirit Father.

[p. 648] **Love** is the desire to do good to others.

[p. 1098] You can best discover values in your associates by discovering their motivation. If some one irritates you, causes feelings of resentment, you should sympathetically seek to discern his viewpoint, his reasons for such objectionable conduct. If once you understand your neighbor, you will become tolerant, and this tolerance will grow into friendship and ripen into **love**.

Love (cont.)

[p. 1098] If you could only know your fellows, you would eventually fall in **love** with them. You cannot truly **love** your fellows by a mere act of the will. **Love** is only born of thoroughgoing understanding of your neighbors' motives and sentiments. It is not so important to love all men today as it is that each day you learn to **love** one more human being. If each day or week you achieve an understanding of one more of your fellows, and if this is the limit of your ability, then you are certainly socializing and truly spiritualizing your personality. **Love** is infectious, and when human devotion is intelligent and wise, love is more catching then hate. But only genuine and unselfish **love** is truly contagious. If each mortal could only become a focus of dynamic affection, this benign virus of **love** would soon pervade the sentimental emotion-stream of humanity, to such an extent that all civilization would be encompassed by **love**, and that would be the realization of the brotherhood of man.

[p. 1574] A father's **love** need not pamper, and it does not condone evil, but it is always anticynical. Fatherly **love** has singleness of purpose, and it always looks for the best in man; that is the attitude of a true parent.

[p. 1575] Fatherly **love** delights in returning good for evil-going good in retaliation for injustice.

[p. 1228] In the true meaning of the word, **love** connotes mutual regard of whole personalities.

[p. 1739] You are destined to live a narrow and mean life if you learn to **love** only those who **love** you. Human **love** may indeed be reciprocal, but divine **love** is outgoing in all its satisfaction-seeking. The less of **love** in any creature's nature, the greater the **love** need, and the more does divine **love** seek to satisfy such need. **Love** is never self-seeking, and it cannot be self-bestowed. Divine **love** cannot be contained; it must be unselfishly bestowed.

[p. 1898] Your inability or unwillingness to forgive your fellows is the measure of your immaturity, your failure to attain adult sympathy, understanding, and **love**. You hold grudges and nurse vengefulness in direct proportion to your ignorance of the inner nature and true longings of your children and your fellow beings. Love is the outworking of the divine and inner urge of life. It is founded on the understanding, nurtured by unselfish service, and perfected in wisdom.

[p. 2018] **Love** is truly contagious and eternally creative. Jesus' death on the cross exemplifies a **love** which is sufficiently strong and divine to forgive sin and swallow up all evil-doing. Jesus disclosed to this world a higher quality of righteousness than justice—mere technical right and wrong. Divine **love** does not merely forgive wrongs; it absorbs and actually destroys them. The forgiveness of **love** utterly transcends the forgiveness of mercy. Mercy sets the guilt of evil-doing to one side; but **love** destroys forever the sin and all weakness resulting therefrom.

[p. 2018] True **love** does not compromise not condone hate; it destroys it. The love of Jesus is never satisfied with mere forgiveness. The Master's **love** implies rehabilitation, eternal survival.

[p. 2019] Greater **love** no man can have than this: that he would be willing to lay down his life for his friends.

[p. 2096] Love is the highest motivation which man may utilize in his universe ascent. But love, divested of truth, beauty, and goodness, is only a sentiment, a

philosophic distortion, a psychic illusion, a spiritual deception. **Love** must always be redefined on successive levels of morontia and spirit progression.

Loyalty, *[p. 51]* Is *loyalty*—devotion to highest duty—desirable? Then must man carry on amid the possibilities of betrayal and desertion. The valor of devotion to duty consists in the implied danger of default.

[p. 435] On the system headquarters the seraphic teachers will further quicken your appreciation of cosmic morality—of the interactions of liberty and **loyalty**. What is **loyalty**? it is the fruit of an intelligent appreciation of universe brotherhood; one could not take so much and give nothing. As you ascend the personality scale, first you learn to be loyal, then to love, then to be filial, and then may you be free: but not until you are a finaliter, not until you have attained perfection of **loyalty**, can you self-realize finality of liberty.

Local Universe, *[p. 166]* One hundred constellations (about 10,000 inhabitable planets) constitute a **local universe**. Each **local universe** has a magnificent architectural headquarters world and is ruled by one of the co-ordinate Creator Sons of God of the order of Michael. Each universe is blessed by the presence of a Union of Days, a representative of the Paradise Trinity.

Luck, *[p. 950]* Bad **luck**—nothing for something—Good **luck**—something for nothing.

[p. 951] **Luck** is merely a term coined to cover the inexplicable in any age of human existence; it designates those phenomena which men are unable or unwilling to penetrate.

M

Magic, *[p. 970]* Civilized man attacks the problems of a real environment through his science; savage man attempted to solve the real problems of an illusory ghost environment by **magic**. **Magic** was the technique of manipulating the conjectured spirit environment whose machinations endlessly explained the inexplicable; it was the art of obtaining voluntary spirit co-operation and of coercing involuntary spirit aid through the use of fetishes or other and more powerful spirits.

[p. 1001] Prayer is not an evolution of magic; they each arose independently. **Magic** was an attempt to adjust Deity to conditions; prayer is the effort to adjust the personality to the will of Deity. True prayer is both moral and religious; **magic** is neither.

Major Sector, *[p. 166]* One hundred minor sectors (about 1,000,000,000 inhabitable worlds) make one **major sector**. Each **major sector** is provided with a superb headquarters and is presided over by three Perfections of Days, Supreme Trinity Personalities.

Man, *[p. 7]* Mortal **man** is very largely an unrealized spiritual potentiality.

[p. 30] God is spirit-spirit personality; **man** is also a spirit-potential spirit personality.

[p. 78] The Eternal Son is wholly spiritual; **man** is very nearly entirely material.

Marriage

[p. 1182] The Adjuster is **man**'s eternity possibility; **man** is the Adjuster's personality possibility.

[p. 1301] Mortal **man** is a machine, a living mechanism; his roots are truly in the physical world of energy. Many human reactions are mechanical in nature; much of life is machinelike. But **man**, a mechanism, is much more than a machine; he is mind endowed and spirit indwelt; and though he can never throughout his material life escape the chemical and electrical mechanics of his existence, he can increasingly learn how to subordinate this physical-life machine to the directive wisdom of experience by the process of consecrating the human mind to the execution of the spiritual urges of the indwelling Thought Adjuster.

[p. 1632] **Man** is the son of God, not a child of the devil.

Marriage, *[p. 915]* **Marriage** is the institutional response of the social organism to the everpresent biologic tension of man's unremitting urge to reproduction-self propagation. Mating is universally natural, and as society evolved from the simple to the complex, there was a corresponding evolution of the mating mores, the genesis of the marital institution. Wherever social evolution has progressed to the stage at which mores are generated, marriage will be found as an evolving institution.

[p. 913] **Marriage**—mating—grows out of bisexuality. **Marriage** is man's reactional adjustment to such bisexuallty, while the family life is the sum total resulting from all such evolutionary and adaptative adjustments. **Marriage** is enduring; it is not inherent in biologic evolution, but it is the basis of all social evolution and is therefore certain of continued existence in some form. **Marriage** has given mankind the home, and the home is the crowning glory of the whole long arduous evolutionary struggle.

[p. 929] **Marriage** which culminates in the home is indeed man's most exalted institution, but it is essentially human; it should never have been called a sacrament.

[p. 930] **Marriage** always has been and still is man's supreme dream of temporal ideality. Though this beautiful dream is seldom realized in its entirety, it endures as a glorious ideal, ever luring progressing mankind on to greater strivings for human happiness. But young men and women should be taught something of the realities of **marriage** before they are plunged into the exacting demands of the interassociations of family life; youthful idealization should be tempered with some degree of premarital disillusionment.

[p. 941] **Marriage**, with children and consequent family life, is stimulative of the highest potentials in human nature and simultaneously provides the ideal avenue for the expression of these quickened attributes of mortal personality.

Materialism, *[p. 646]* Hence **materialism**, atheism, is the maximum ugliness, the climax of the finite antithesis of the beautiful.

[p. 2077] **Materialism** reduces man to a soulless automaton and constitutes him merely an arithmetical symbol finding a helpless place in the mathematical formula of an unromantic and mechanistic universe.

Matter, *[p. 140]* Organized energy which is subject to linear gravity except as it is modified by motion and conditioned by mind.

[p. 472] Light, heat, electricity, magnetism, chemism, energy, and **matter** are—in origin, nature, and destiny—one and the same thing, together with other material realities as yet undiscovered on Urantia.

[p. 648] Physical *matter* is the time-space shadow of the Paradise energy-shining of the absolute deities.

Maturity, *[p. 1295]* In the **maturity** of the developing self, the past and future are brought together to illuminate the true meaning of the present. As the self matures, it reaches further and further back into the past for experience, while its wisdom forecasts seek to penetrate deeper and deeper into the unknown future. And as the conceiving self extends this reach ever further into both past and future, so does judgement become less and less dependent on the momentary present.

[p. 1295] To become mature is to live more intensely in the present, at the same time escaping from the limitations of the present. The plans of **maturity**, founded on past experience, are coming into being in the present is such manner as to enhance the values of the future.

[p. 1296] The time unit of **maturity** is proportioned so to reveal the co-ordinate relationship of past-present-future that the self begins to gain insight into the wholeness of events, begins to view the landscape of time from the panoramic perspective of broadened horizons, begins perhaps to suspect the nonbeginning, nonending eternal continuum, the fragments of which are called time.

Meaning, *[p. 1097]* **Meaning** is something which experience adds to value; it is the appreciative consciousness of values. An isolated and purely selfish pleasure may connote a virtual devaluation of **meanings**, a meaningless enjoyment bordering on relative evil.

[p. 1220] **Meanings** are derived from a combination of recognition and understanding. **Meanings** are nonexistent in a wholly sensory or material world. **Meanings** and values are only perceived in the inner or supermaterial spheres of human experience.

Meekness, *[p. 1574]* Genuine **meekness** has no relation to fear. It is rather an attitude of man co-operating with God— "Your will be done." It embraces patience and forbearance and is motivated by an unshakable faith in a lawful and friendly universe. It masters all temptations to rebel against the divine leading. Jesus was the ideal meek man of Urantia, and he inherited a vast universe.

Mercy, *[p. 38]* **Mercy** is simply justice tempered by that wisdom which grows out of perfection of knowledge and the full recognition of the natural weaknesses and environmental handicaps of finite creatures.

[p. 38] **Mercy** is the natural and inevitable offspring of goodness and love. The good nature of a loving Father could not possibly withhold the wise ministry of mercy to each member of every group of his universe children. Eternal justice and divine **mercy** together constitute what is human experience would be called fairness.

Divine **mercy** represents a, fairness technique, of adjustment between the universe levels of perfection and imperfection. **Mercy** is not a contravention of justice but rather an understanding interpretation of the demands of supreme justice as it is fairly applied to the subordinate spiritual beings and to the material creatures of the evolving universes.

Mercy (cont.)

[p. 115] Justice is the collective thought of righteousness; **mercy** is its personal expression. **Mercy** is the attitude of love.

[p. 314] The Memory of **Mercy** is a living trial balance, a current statement of your account with the supernatural forces of the realms.

[p. 314] The Memory of **Mercy** must show that the saving credit established by the Sons of God has been fully and faithfully paid out in the loving ministry of the patient personalities of the Third Source and Center. But when **mercy** is exhausted, when the "memory" thereof testifies to its depletion, then does justice prevail and righteousness decree. For **mercy** is not to be thrust upon those who despise it; **mercy** is not a gift to be trampled underfoot by the persistent rebels of time. Nevertheless, though **mercy** is thus precious and dearly bestowed, your individual drawing credits are always far in excess of your ability to exhaust the reserve if you are sincere of purpose and honest of heart.

[p. 315] You should realize that there is a great reward of personal satisfaction in being first just. next fair, then patient, then kind. And then, on that foundation, if you choose, and have it in your heart, you can take the next step and really show **mercy**; but you cannot exhibit mercy in and of itself. These steps must be traversed; otherwise there can be no genuine **mercy**. There may be patronage, condescension, or charity—even pity—but not **mercy**. True **mercy** comes only as the beautiful climax to these preceding adjuncts to group understanding, mutual appreciation, fraternal fellowship, spiritual communion, and divine harmony.

[p. 1575] "Happy are the merciful, for they shall obtain **mercy**." **Mercy** here denotes the height and depth and breadth of the truest friendship—loving-kindness. **Mercy** sometimes may be passive, but here it is active and dynamic—supreme fatherliness.

[p. 2018] The forgiveness of love utterly transcends the forgiveness of **mercy**. **Mercy** sets the guilt of evil-doing to one side; but love destroys forever the sin and all weakness resulting therefrom.

Metaphysics, *[p. 1136]* But many mortals have recognized the desirability of having some, method of reconciling the interplay between the widely separated domains of science and religion? and **metaphysics** is the result of man's unavailing attempt to span this well-recognized chasm. But human metaphysics has proved more confusing than illiminating. **Metaphysics** stands for man's well-meant but futile effort to compensate for the absence of the mota of morontia.

[p. 1139] Always, in the absence of revelation or in the failure to accept or grasp it, has mortal man resorted to his futile gesture of **metaphysics**, that being the only human substitute for the revelation of truth or for the mota of morontia personality.

Midsoniters, *[p. 400]* The progeny of a Melchizedek life carrier and a Material Daughter are known as **midsoniters**.

Militarism, *[p. 786]* **Militarism** is autocratic and cruel— savage. It promotes social organization among the conquerors but disintegrates the vanquished.

Do not make the mistake of glorifying war; rather discern what it has done for society so that you may the more accurately visualize what its substitutes must provide in order to continue the advancement of civilization. And if such adequate substitutes are not provided, then you may be sure that war will long continue.

Mile, *[p. 519]* The standard **mile** of Jerusem is equivalent to about seven Urantia miles.

Milky Way, *[p. 475]* The densest plane of the superuniverse, the **Milky Way**, which is also the densest plane of the outer universes.

Mind, *[p. 9]* Any and all that responds to the mind circuit of the Conjoint Actor, we call **mind**, **mind** as an attribute of the Infinite Spirit—**mind** in all its phases.

[p. 9] **Mind** is a phenomenon connoting the presence-activity of living ministry in addition to varied energy systems; and this is true on all levels of intelligence. In personality, mind ever intervenes between spirit and matter; therefore is the universe illuminated by three kinds of light; material light, intellectual insight, and spirit luminosity.

[p. 8] Mind; The thinking, perceiving, and feeling mechanism of the human organism. The total conscious and unconscious experience. The intelligence associated with the emotional life reaching upward through worship and wisdom to the spirit level.

[p. 102] **Mind** transmutes the values of spirit into the meanings of intellect; volition has power to bring the meanings of mind to fruit in both the material and spiritual domains. The Paradise ascent involves a relative and differential growth in spirit, mind, and energy. The personality is the unifier of these components of experiential individuality.

[p. 103] **Mind**, on Urantia, is a compromise between the essence of thought perfection and the evolving mentality of your immature human nature. Mind is truly of divine origin, and it does have a divine destiny, but your mortal **minds** are not yet of divine dignity.

[p. 140] **Mind** is the technique whereby spirit realities become experiential to creature personalities. And in the last analysis the unifying possibilities of even human **mind**, the ability to co-ordinate things, ideas, and values, is supermaterial.

[p. 403] **Mind** is a divinity bestowal, but it is not immortal when it functions without spirit insight, and when it is devoid of the ability to worship and crave survival.

[p. 1216] Material **mind** is the arena in which human personalities live, are self conscious, make decisions, choose God or forsake him, eternalize or destroy themselves. Material evolution has provided you a life machine, your body; the Father himself has endowed you with the purest spirit reality known in the universe, your Thought Adjuster. But into your hands, subject to your own decisions, has been given **mind**, and it is by **mind** that you live or die. It is within this **mind** and with this **mind** that you make those moral decisions which enable you to achieve Adjusterlikeness, and that is Godlikeness.

Mortal **mind** is a temporary intellect system loaned to human beings for use during a material lifetime, and as they use this **mind**, they are either accenting or rejecting the potential of eternal existence. **Mind** is about all you have of universe reality that is subject to your will, and the soul—the morontia self—will faithfully portray the harvest of the temporal decisions which the mortal self is making.

[p. 1217] **Mind** is the cosmic instrument on which the human will can play the discords of destruction, or upon which this same human will can bring forth the exquisite melodies of God identification and consequent eternal survival.

Mind, Cosmic

[p. 1217] The material **mind** of mortal man is the cosmic loom that carries the morontia fabrics on which the indwelling Thought Adjuster threads the spirit patterns of a universe character of enduring values and divine meanings—a surviving soul of ultimate destiny and unending career, a potential finaliter.

[p. 1733] While the **mind** is not the seat of the spiritual nature, it is indeed the gateway thereto.

Mind, Cosmic, *[p. 481] The cosmic mind.* This is the sevenfold diversified mind of time and space, one phase of which is ministered by each of the Seven Master Spirits to one of the seven superuniverses. The **cosmic mind** encompasses all finite-mind levels and co-ordinates experientially with the evolutionary-deity levels of the Supreme Mind and Transcendentally with the existential levels of absolute mind— the direct circuits of the Conjoint Actor.

Minor Sector, *[p. 166] The Minor Sector.* One hundred local universes (about 1,000,000,000 inhabitable planets) constitute a **minor sector** of the super universe government; it has a wonderful headquarters world, wherefrom its rulers, the Recents of Days, administer the affairs of the **minor sector.** There are three Recents of Days, Supreme Trinity Personalities, on each **minor sector** headquarters.

Monogamy, *[p. 781]* Polygamy is the survival of the female-slavery element in marriage. **Monogamy** is the slave-free ideal of the matchless association of one man and one woman in the ex quisite enterprise of home building, offspring rearing, mutual culture, and self improvement.

[p. 927] **Monogamy** always has been, now is, and forever will be the idealistic goal of human sex evolution. This ideal of true pair marriage entails self-denial, and therefore does it so often fail just because one or both of the contracting parties are deficient in that acme of all human virtues, rugged self-control.

Monota, *[p. 471] Monota.* Energy is close of kin to divinity when it is Paradise energy. We incline to the belief that **monota** is the living, nonspirit energy of Paradise—an eternity counterpart of the living, spirit energy of the Original Son—hence the nonspiritual energy system of the Universal Father.

Morality, *[p. 193]* **Morality** can never be advanced by law or by force. It is a personal and freewill matter and must be disseminated by the contagion of the contact of morally fragrant persons with those who are less morally responsive, but who are also desirous of doing the Father's will.

Moral acts are those human performances which are characterized by the highest intelligence, directed by selective discrimination in the choice of superior ends as well as in the selection of moral means to attain these ends. Such conduct is virtuous. Supreme virtue, then, is wholeheartedly to choose to do the will of the Father in heaven.

[p. 2096] **Morality** is the essential pre-existent soil of personal God-consciousness, the personal realization of the Adjuster's inner presence, but such **morality** is not the source of religious experience and the resultant spiritual insight. The moral nature is superanimal but subspiritual. **Morality** is equivalent to the recognition of duty, the realization of the existence of right and wrong. The moral zone intervenes between the animal and the human types of mind as morontia functions between the material and the spiritual spheres of personality attainment.

Mota

The evolutionary mind is able to discover law, morals, and ethics; but -the bestowed spirit, the indwelling Adjuster, reveals to the evolving human mind the lawgiver, the Fathersource of all that is true, beautiful, and good; and such an illuminated man has a religion and is spiritually equipped to begin the long and adventurous search for God.

Morality is not necessarily spiritual; it may be wholly and purely human, albeit real religion enhances all moral values, makes them more meaningful. **Morality** without religion fails to reveal ultimate goodness, and it also fails to provide for the survival of even its own moral values. Religion provides for the enhancement, glorification, and assured survival of everything **morality** recognizes and approves.

Morontia, *[p. 9]* Morontia is a term designating a vast level intervening between the material and the spiritual. It may designate personal or Impersonal realities, living or nonliving energies. The warp of morontia is spiritual; its woof is physical.

Mortal, God-conscious, *[p. 1740]* The **God-conscious mortal** is certain of salvation; he is unafraid of life; he is honest and consistent. He knows how bravely to endure unavoidable suffering; he is uncomplaining when faced by inescapable hardship.

The true believer does not grow weary in well-doing just because he is thwarted. Difficulty whets the ardor of the truth lover, while obstacles only challenge the exertions of the undaunted kingdom builder.

Mota, *[p. 518]* **Mota**-morontia wisdom.

[p. 554] **Mota** is more than a superior philosophy; it is to philosophy as two eyes are to one; it has a stereoscopic effect on meanings and values. Material man sees the universe, as it were, with but one eye——flat. Mansion world students achieve cosmic perspective——depth——by superimposing the perceptions of the morontia life upon the perseptions of the physical life,.

[p. 1136] Reason is the understanding technique of the sciences; faith is the insight technique of religion; mota is the technique of the morontia level. **Mota** is a supermaterial reality sensitivity which is beginning to compensate incomplete growth, having for its substance knowledge-reason and for its essence faith-insight. **Mota** is a super-philosphical reconciliation of divergent reality perception which is nonattainable by material personalities; it is predicated, in part, on the experience of having survived the material life of the flesh. But many mortals have recognized the desirability of having some method of reconciling the interplay between the widely separated domains of science and religion; and metaphysics is the result of man's unavailing attempt to span this well-recognized chasm. But human metaphysics has proved more confusing than illuminating. Metaphysics stands for man's well-meant but futile effort to compensate for the absence of the **mota** of morontia.

[p. 1137] Revelation is evolutionary man's only hope of bridging the morontia gulf. Faith and reason, unaided my **mota**, cannot conceive and construct a logical universe. Without the insight of mota, mortal man cannot discern goodness, love, and truth in the phenomena of the material world.

Mysticism

Mysticism, *[p. 1121]* Religion is evolutionary man's supreme endowment the one thing which enables him to carry on and "endure as seeing Him who is Invisible." **Mysticism**, however, is often something of a retreat from life which is embraced by those humans who do not relish the more robust activities of living a religious life in the open arenas of human society and commerce. True religion must *act*.

Nature, [p. 56] **Nature** is in a limited sense the physical habit of God

*[p. 56]*Therefore, **nature**, as mortal man understands it, presents the underlying foundation and fundamental background of a changeless Deity and his immutable laws, modified by, fluctuating because of, and experiencing upheavals through, the Working of the local plans, purposes, patterns, and conditions which have been Inaugurated and are being carried out by the local universe, constellation, system, and planetary forces and personalities.

[p. 56] **Nature** is a time-space resultant of two cosmic factors: first, the immutability, perfection, and rectitude of Paradise Deity, and second, the experimental plans, executive blunders, insurrectionary errors, incompleteness of development, and imperfection of wisdom of the extra-Paradise creatures from the highest to the lowest.

[p. 56] **Nature** therefore carries a uniform, unchanging, majestic, and marvelous thread of perfection from the circle of eternity; but in each universe, on each planet, and in each individual life, this **nature** is modified, qualified, and perchance marred by the acts, the mistakes, and the disloyalties of the creatures of the evolutionary systems and universes; and therefore must nature ever be of a changing mood, whimsical withal, though stable underneath, and varied in accordance with the operating procedures of a local universe.

Nature is the perfection of paradise divided by the incompletion, evil, and sin of the unfinished universes. This quotient is thus expressive of both the perfect and the partial, of both the eternal and the temporal. Continuing evolution modifies nature by augmenting the content of paradise perfection and by diminishing the content of the evil, error, and disharmony of relative reality.

God is not personally present in **nature** or in any of the forces of nature, for the phenomenon of nature is the superimposition of the imperfections of progressive evolution and, sometimes, the consequences of insurrectionary rebellion, upon the Paradise foundations of God's universal law. As it appears on such a world as Urantia, **nature** can never be the adequate expression, the true representation, the faithful portrayal, of an all-wise and infinite God.

Nature, on your world, is a qualification of the laws of perfection by the evolutionary plans of the local universe. What a travesty to worship **nature** because it is in a limited, qualified sense pervaded by God; because it Is a phase of the universal and, therefore, divine power! **Nature** is also a manifestation of the unfinished, the incomplete, the imperfect outworkings of the development, growth, and progress of a universe experiment in cosmic evolution.

The apparent defects of the natural world are not indicative of any such corresponding defects in the character of God.

[p. 56] No, **nature** is not God. **Nature** is not an object of worship.

Nature, animal, *[p. 2017]* The **animal nature**—the tendency toward evildoing—may be hereditary, but sin is not transmitted from parent to child.

O

Original, The, *[p. 1262]* **The Original.** The unqualified concept of the First Source and Center, that source manifestation of the I AM from which all reality takes origin.

 [p. 1262] **The Original** is that which is.

P

Paradise, *[p. 7]* **Paradise** is a term inclusive of the personal and the nonpersonal focal Absolutes of all phases of universe reality. **Paradise**, properly, qualified, may connote any and all forms of reality. Deity, divinity, personality, and energy—spiritual, mindal, or material. All share **Paradise** as the place of origin, function, and destiny, as regards values, meanings, and factual existence.

Paradise, The Isle of, *[p. 7]* Paradise not otherwise qualified— is the Absolute of the material-gravity control of the First Source and Ctnter. Paradise is motionless, being the only stationary thing in the universe of universes. The **Isle of Paradise** has a universe location but no position in space. This eternal Isle is the actual source of the physical universes, past, present, and future. The nuclear Isle of Light is a Deity derivative, but it is hardly Deity; neither are the material creations a part of Deity; they are a consequence.

 Paradise is not a creator; it is a unique controller of many universe activities, far more of a controller than a reactor. Throughout the material universes paradise influences the reactions and conduct of all beings having to do with force, energy, and power, but Paradise itself is unique, exclusive, and isolated in the universes. Paradise represents nothing and nothing represents Paradise. It is neither a force nor a presence; it is just *Paradise.*

 [p. 8] But the **Isle of Paradise** is nonpersonal and extraspiritual, being the essence of the universal body, the source and center of physical matter, and the absolute master pattern of universal reality.

 [p. 101] Paradise is the pattern of infinity; the God of Action is the activator of that pattern. Paradise is the material fulcrum of infinity;

 [p. 118] Paradise is the eternal center of the universe of universes and the abiding place of the Universal Father, the Eternal Son, the Infinite Spirit, and their divine co-ordinates and associates. This central Isle is the most gigantic organized body of cosmic reality in all the master universe. Paradise is a material sphere as well as a spiritual abode. All of the intelligent creation of the Universal Father is domiciled on material abodes; hence must the absolute controlling center also be material, literal. And again it should be reiterated that spirit things and spiritual beings are *real.*

Paradise, the Isle of (cont.)

The material, beauty of Paradise consists in the magnificence of its physical perfection; the grandeur of the Isle of God is exhibited in the superb intellectual accomplishments and mind development of its inhabitants; the glory of the central Isle is shown forth in the infinite endowment of divine spirit personality—the light of life. But the depths of the spiritual beauty and the wonders of this magnificent ensemble are utterly beyond the comprehension of the finite mind of material creatures. The glory and spiritual splendor of the divine abode are impossible of mortal comprehension. And Paradise is from eternity; there are neither records nor traditions respecting the origin of this nuclear Isle of Light and Life.

[p. 126] Paradise is the geographic center of infinity; it is not a part of universal creation, not even a real part of the eternal Havona universe. We commonly refer to the central Isle as belonging to the divine universe, but it really does not. Paradise is an eternal and exclusive existence.

[p. 127] Paradise is not ancestral to any being or living entity; it is not a creator. Personality and mind-spirit relationships are transmissible, but pattern is not, Patterns are never reflections; they are duplications— reproductions. Paradise is the absolute of patterns; Havona is an exhibit of these potentials in actuality.

God's residence is central and eternal, glorious and ideal. His home is the beauteous pattern for all universe headquarters worlds; and the central universe of his immediate indwelling is the pattern for all universes in the ideals, organization, and ultimate destiny.

Paradise is the universal headquarters of all personality activities and the source-center of all force-space and energy manifestations. Everything which has been, now is, or is yet to be, has come, now comes, or will come forth from this central abiding place of the eternal Gods. Paradise is the center of all creation, the source of all energies, and the place of primal origin of all personalities.

[p. 637] And Paradise is the actual source of all material universespast, present, and future. But this cosmic derivation is an *eternity* event; at no *time*—past, present, or future— does either space of the material cosmos come forth from the nuclear Isle of Light. As the cosmic source, Paradise functions prior to space and before time; hence would its derivations seem to be orphaned in time and space did they not emerge through the Unqualified Absolute, their ultimate repository in space and their revealer and regulator in time.

Pattern, *[p. 10]* **Pattern** is a master design from which copies are made. Eternal Paradise is the absolute of **patterns**; the Eternal Son is the **pattern** personality; the Universal rather is the direct ancestor-source of both. But Paradise does not bestow **pattern**, and the Son cannot bestow personality.

[p. 10] But **pattern** is **pattern** and remains **pattern**; only *copies* are multiplied.

Peace, *[p. 783]* War is the natural state and heritage of evolving man; **peace** is the social yardstick measuring civilization's advancement.

*[p. 783]*War is an animalistic reaction to misunderstandings and irritations; **peace** attends upon the civilized solution of all such problems and difficulties.

Peace, Jesus, [p. 1954] The **peace of Jesus** is the joy and satisfaction of a God-knowing individual who has achieved the triumph of learning fully how to do the will of God while living the mortal life in the flesh.

[p. 1955] The **peace of Jesus** is, then, the peace and assurance of a son who fully believes that his career for time and eternity is safely and wholly in the care and keeping of an all-wise, all-loving, and all-powerful spirit Father. And this is, indeed, a peace which passes the understanding of mortal mind, but which can be enjoyed to the full by the believing human heart.

Peacemaking, *[p. 1575]* **Peacemaking** is the cure of distrust and suspicion.

Perfections of Days, *[p. 179]* The rulers of the Superuniverse major sectors.

Personal, *[p. 9]* Any and all things responding to the personality circuit of the Father, we call **personal**.

Personality, *[p. 8]* **Personality** is never spontaneous; it is the gift of the Paradise Father. **Personality** is superimposed upon energy, and it is associated only with living energy system identity can be associated with nonliving energy patterns.

The Universal Father is the secret of the reality of **personality** the bestowal of **personality**, and the destiny of **personality**. The Eternal Son is the absolute **personality**, the secret of spiritual energy morontia spirits, and perfected spirits. The Conjoint Actor is the spirit-mind personality, the source of intelligence, reason, and the universal mind.

[p. 9] The **personality** of mortal man is neither body, mind, nor spirit; neither is it the soul. **Personality** is the one changeless reality in an otherwise ever-changing creature experiences and it unifies all other associated factors of individuality. The **personality** is the unique bestowal which the Universal Father makes upon the living and associated energies of matter, mind, and spirit, and which survives with the survival of the morontial soul.

[p. 29] In the contemplation of Deity, the concept of **personality** must be divested of the idea of corporeality. A material body is not indispensable to **personality** in either man or God. The corporeality error is shown in both extremes of human philosophy. In materialism, since man loses his body at death, he ceases to exist as a **personality**; in pantheism, since God has no body, he is not, therefore, a person. The superhuman type of progressing personality functions in a union of mind and spirit.

Personality is not simply an attribute of God; it rather stands for the totality of the co-ordinated infinite nature and the unified divine will which is exhibited in eternity and universality of perfect expression. **Personality**, in the supreme sense, is the revelation of God to the universe of universes.

[p. 70] **Personality** is one of the unsolved mysteries of the universes. We are able to form adequate concepts of the factors entering into the make-up of various orders and levels of **personality**, but we do not fully comprehend the real nature of the **personality** itself. We clearly perceive the numerous factors which, when put together, constitute the vehicle for human personality, but we do not fully comprehend the nature and significance of such a finite **personality**.

Personality is potential in all creatures who possess a mind endowment ranging from the minimum of self-consciousness to the maximum of God-consciousness. But mind endowment alone is not **personality**, neither is spirit nor physical energy. **Personality** is that quality and value in cosmic reality which is exclusively bestowed by God the Father upon these living systems of the associated and

Personality (cont.)

coordinated energies of matter, mind, and spirit. Neither is personality a progressive achievement. **Personality** may be material or spiritual, but there either is **personality** or there is no **personality**.

[p. 194] **Personality** is a unique endowment of original nature whose existence is independent of, and antecedent to, the bestowal of the Thought Adjuster. Nevertheless, the presence of the Adjuster does augment the qualitative manifestation of **personality**. Thought Adjuster, when they come forth from the Father, are identical in nature, but personality is diverse, original, and exclusive; and the manifestation of **personality** is further conditioned and qualified by the nature and qualities of the associated energies of a material, mindal, and spiritual nature which constitute the organismal vehicle for personality manifestation.

Personalities may be similar, but they are never the same. Persons of a given series, type, order, or pattern may and do resemble one another, but they are never identical. **Personality** is that feature of an individual which we *know*, and which enables us to identify such a being at some future time regardless of the nature and extent of changes inform, mind, or spirit status.

Personality is that part of any individual which enables us to recognize and positively identify that person as the one we have previously known, no matter how much he may have changed because of modification of the vehicle of expression and manifestation of his **personality**.

[p. 29] Human **personality** is the time-space image-shadow cast by the divine Creator **personality**. And no actuality can ever be adequately comprehended by an examination of its shadow. Shadows should be interpreted in terms of the true substance.

[p. 236] **Personality** is designed and bestowed by the Universal Father.

[p. 1434] **Personality** is that cosmic endowment, that chase of universal reality, which can coexist with unlimited change and at the same time retain its identity in the very presence of all such changes, and forever afterward.

Pharisees, [p. 1534] The scribes and rabbis, taken together, were called **Pharisees**. They referred to themselves as the "associates". In many ways they were the progressive group among the Jews, having adopted many teachings not clearly found in the Hebrew scriptures, such as belief in the resurrection of the dead, a doctrine only mentioned by a later prophet, Daniel.

Philosophy, [p. 2096] **Philosophy** is man's attempt at the unification of human experience.

Pleasure, [p. 51] The satisfaction of happiness.

Polygamy, [p. 781] **Polygamy** is the survival of the female-slavery element in marriage.

Position, [p. 776] Social and political prestige.

Power, [p. 776] The craving to be master.

[p. 9] **Power** is ordinarily limited to the designation of the electronic level of material or linear-gravity-responsive matter in the grand universe. **Power** is also employed to designate sovereignty.

Power, Universe, [p. 9] **Universe power** includes all forms of energy which, while still responding to Paradise gravity, are directly responsive to linear gravity. This is the electronic level of energy-matter and all subsequent evolutions thereof.

Prayer

[p. 470] Space-force has been changed into space-energy and thence into the energy of gravity control. Thus has physical energy been ripened to that point where it can be directed into channels of power and made to serve the manifold purposes of the universe Creators.

On Uversa we refer to the realm of **universe power** as GRAVITA.

Prayer, [p. 996] The truest **prayer** is in reality a communion between man and his Maker.

[p. 997] And thus does **prayer** function as the most potent agency of religion in the conservation of the highest values and ideals of those who pray.

[p. 997] **Prayer** ever has been and ever will be a twofold human experience; a phychologic procedure interassociated with a spiritual technique.

[p. 998] When the **prayer** seeks nothing for the one who prays nor anything for his fellows, then such attitudes of the soul tend to the levels of true worship.

[p. 999] **Prayer** is the technique whereby, sooner or later, every religion becomes institutionalized, and in time **prayer** becomes associated with numerous secondary agencies, some helpful, others decidedly deleterious, such as priests, holy books, worship rituals, and ceremonials.

[p. 999] Do not be so slothful as to ask God to solve your difficulties, but never hesitate to ask him for wisdom and spiritual strangth to guide and sustain you while you yourself resolutely and courageously attack the problems at hand.

[p. 1001] **Prayer** is not an evolution of magic; they each arose independently. True **prayer** is both moral and religious; magic is neither.

[p. 1002] Genuine **prayer** adds to spiritual growth, modifies attitudes, and yields that satisfaction which comes from communion with divinity. It is a spontaneous outburst of God-consciousness.

God answers man's **prayer** by giving him an increased revelation of truth, an enhanced appreciation of beauty, and an augmented concept of goodness. **Prayer** is a subjective gesture, but it contacts with mighty objective realities on the spiritual levels of human experience; It is a meaningful reach by the human for superhuman values. It is the most potent spiritual-growth stimulus.

Words are irrelevant to **prayer**; they are merely the intellectual channel in which the river of spiritual supplication may chance to flow. The word value of a **prayer** is purely auto-suggestive in private devotions and sociosuggestive in group devotions. God answers the soul's attitude, not the words.

Prayer is not a technique of escape from conflict but rather a stimulus to growth in the very face of conflict. Pray only for values, not things; for growth, not for gratification.

[p. 1123] **Prayer** is indeed a part of religious experience, but it has been wrongly emphasized by modern religions, much to the neglect of the more essential communion of worship. The reflective powers of the mind are deepened and broadened by worship. **Prayer** may enrich the life, but worship illuminates destiny.

[p. 1616] **Prayer** is designed to make man less thinking but more *realizing*; it is not designed to increase knowledge but rather to expand insight.

[p. 1616] **Prayer** is self-reminding——sublime thinking; worship is self-forgetting——superthinking. Worship is effortless attention, true and ideal soulrest, a form of restful spiritual exertion.

Prayer (cont.)

[p. 1618] **Prayer** is entirely a personal and spontaneous expression of the attitude of the soul toward the spirit; prayer should be the communion of sonship and the expression of fellowship. **Prayer**, when indited by the spirit, leads to co-operative spiritual progress. The ideal **prayer** is a form of spiritual communion which leads to intelligent worship. True braying is the sincere attitude of reaching heavenward for the attainment of your ideals.

[p. 1619] **Prayer** is the breath of the soul and should lead you to be persistent in your attempt to ascertain the Father's will.

[p. 1621] **Prayer** is the breath of the spirit life in the midst of the material civilization of the races of mankind. Worship is salvation for the pleasure-seeking generations of mortals. As **prayer** may be likened to recharging the spiritual batteries of the soul, so worship may be compared to the act of tuning in the soul to catch the universe broadcasts of the infinite spirit of the Universal Father. **Prayer** is the sincere and longing look of the child to its spirit Father; it is a psychologic process of exchanging the human will for the divine will. **Prayer** is a part of the divine plan for making over that which is into that which ought to be.

[p. 1848] THE ANSWER TO **PRAYER**

1. **Prayer** is an expression of the finite mind in an effort to approach the Infinite. The making of a prayer must, therefore be limited by the knowledge, widsom, and attributes of the of the finite; likewise must the answer be conditioned by the vision, aims, ideals, and prerogatives of the Infinite. There never can be observed an unbroken continuity of material phenomena between the making of a **prayer** and the reception of the full spiritual answer thereto.

2. When a **prayer** is apparently unanswered, the delay often betokens a better answer, although one which is for some good reason greatly delayed. No sincere **prayer** is denied an answer except when the superior viewpoint of the spiritual world has devised a better answer, an answer which meets the petition of the spirit of man as contrasted with the **prayer** of the mere mind of man.

3. The **prayers** of time, when indited by the spirit and expressed in faith, are often so vast and all-encompassing that they can be answered only in eternity; the finite petition is sometimes so graught with the grasp of the Infinite that the answer must long be postponed to await the creation of adequate capacity for receptivity; the **prayer** of faith may be so all-embracing that the answer can be received only on Paradise.

4. The answers to the **prayer** of the mortal mind are often of such a nature that they can be received and recognized only after that same praying mind has attained the Immortal state. The **prayer** of the material being can many times be answered only when such an individual has progressed to the spirit level.

5. The **prayer** of a God-knowing person may be so distorted by ignorance and so deformed by superstition that the answer thereto would be highly undesirable. Then must the intervening spirit beings so translate such a **prayer** that, when the answer arrives, the petitioner wholly fails to recognize it as the answer to his **prayer**.

6. All true **prayers** are addressed to spiritual beings, and all such petitions must be answered in spiritual terms, and all such answers must consist in spiritual realities. Spirit beings cannot bestow material answers to the spirit petitions of even material beings. Material beings can pray effectively only when they "pray in the spirit".

7. No **prayer** can hope for an answer unless it is born of the spirit and nurtured by faith. Your sincere faith implies that you have in advance virtually granted your **prayer** hearers the full right to answer your petitions in accordance with that supreme wisdom and that divine love which your faith depicts as always actuating those beings to whom you pray.

8. The child is always within his rights when he presumes to petition the parent; and the parent is always within his parental obligations to the immature child when his superior wisdom dictates that the answer to the child's **prayer** be delayed, modified, segregated, transcended, or postponed to another stage of spiritual ascension.

*[p. 1849]*9. Do not hesitate to pray the **prayers** of spirit longing; doubt not that you shall receive the answer to your petitions. These answers will be on deposit, awaiting your achievement of those future spiritual levels of actual cosmic attainment, on this world or on others, whereon it will become possible, for you to recognize and appropriate the long-waiting answers to your earlier but illtimed petitions.

10. All genuine spirit-born petitions are certain of an answer. Ask and you shall receive. But you should remember that you are progressive creatures of time and space; therefore must you constantly reckon with the time-space factor in the experience of your personal reception of the full answers to your manifold **prayers** and petitions.

Prejudice, *[p. 1774]* **Prejudice** blinds the soul to the recognition of truth and **prejudice** can be removed only by the sincere devotion of the soul to the adoration of a cause that is all-embracing and all-inclusive of one's fellow men. **Prejudice** is inseparably linked to selfishness. **Prejudice** can be eliminated only by the abandonment of self-seeking and by substituting therefor the quest of the satisfaction of the service of a cause that is not only greater than self, but one that is even greater than all humanity— the search for God, the attainment of divinity. The evidence of maturity of personality consists in the Transformation of human desire so that it constantly seeks for the realization of those values which are highest and most divinely real.

Pride, *[p. 1223]* Of all the dangers which beset man's mortal nature and Jeopardize his spiritual integrity, **pride**. is the greatest.

[p. 1223] **Pride** is deceitful, intoxicating, and sin-breeding whether found in an individual, a group, a race, or a nation. It is literally true, "**Pride** goes before a fall."

R

Ransomer, *[p. 2017]* Though it is hardly proper to speak of Jesus as a sacrificer, a **ransomer**, or a redeemer, it is wholly correct to refer to him as a *savior*.

Reality, [p. 5] **Reality**, as comprehended by finite beings, is partial, relative, and shadowy.

(6) **Reality** differentially actualizes on diverse universe levels; **reality** originates in and by the infinite volition of the Universal Father and is realizable in three primal phases on many different levels of universe actualization:

1. Undeified **reality**

2. Deified **reality**

3. Interassociated **reality**

Reason

Reason, *[p. 1106]* **Reason** is the method of science; faith is the method of religion; logic is the attempted technique of philosophy.

[p. 1106] **Reason**, through the study of science, may lead back through nature to a First Cause, but it requires religious faith to transform the First Cause of science into a God of salvation; and revelation is further required for the validation of such a faith, such spiritual insight.

[p. 1106] **Reason** is the proof of science, faith the proof of religion, logic the proof of philosophy, but revelation is validated only by human experience.

[p. 1136] **Reason** is the understanding technique of the sciences: faith is the insight technique of religions mota is the technique of the morontia level.

[p. 1139] **Reason** is the act of recognizing the conclusions of consciousness with regard to the experience in and with the physical world of energy and matter.

Recents of Days, *[p. 179]* The directors of the Superuniverse minor sectors.

Recognition, *[p. 1219]* **Recognition** is the intellectual process of fitting the sensory impressions received from the external world into the memory patterns of the individual.

Redeemer, *[p. 2017]* Though it is hardly proper to speak of Jesus as a sacrificer, a ransomer, or a **redeemer**, it is wholly correct to refer to him as a *savior*. He forever made the way of salvation (survival) more clear and certain; he did better and, more surely show the way of salvation for all the mortals of all the worlds of the universe of Nebadon.

Reflectivity, *[p. 105]* This is the phenomenon of *universe* **reflectivity**, that unique and inexplicable power to see, hear, sense, and know all things as they transpire throughout a superuniverse, and to focalize, by **reflectivity**, all this information and knowledge at any desired point.

[p. 105] **Reflectivity** appears to be omniscience within the limits of the experiential finite and may represent the emergence of the presence-consciousness of the Supreme Being.

Religion, *[p. 67]* The **religion** of Jesus *is* salvation from self, deliverance from the evils of creature isolation in time and in eternity.

[p. 68] **Religion** is not grounded in the facts of science, the obligations of society, the assumptions of philosophy, or the implied duties of morality. **Religion** is an independent realm of human response to life situations and is unfailingly exhibited at all stages of human development which are postmoral. **Religion** may permeate all four levels of the realization of values and the enjoyment of universe fellowship: the physical or material level of self-preservation; the social or emotional level of fellowships the moral or duty level of reason; the spiritual level of the consciousness of universe fellowship through divine worship.

[p. 1006] **Religion** fostered civilization and provided societal continuity; it has been the moral police force of all time. **Religion** provided that human disciscourge of evolution which ruthlessly drives indolent and suffering humanity from its natural state of intellectual inertia forward and upward to the higher levels of reason and wisdom.

[p. 1095] **Religion** cannot be bestowed, received, loaned, learned, or lost. It is a personal experience which grows proportionally to the growing quest for final values.

Religion

[p. 1123] Revealed **religion** is the unifying element of human existence. Revelation unifies history, co-ordinates geology, astronomy, physics, chemistry, biology, sociology, and psychology.

[p. 1128] True **religion** has nothing to do with alleged miracles, and never does revealed **religion** point to miracles as proof of authority. **Religion** is ever and always rooted and grounded in personal experience.

[p. 1132] **Religion** is designed to change man's environment, but much of the **religion** found among mortals today has become helpless to do this. Environment has all too often mastered **religion**.

Remember that in the **religion** of all ages the experience which is paramount is the feeling regarding moral values and social meanings, not the thinking regarding theologic dogmas or philosophic theories.**Religion** evolves favorably as the element of magic is replaced by the concept of morals.

[p. 1124] The relation between the creature and the Creator is a living experience, a dynamic religious faith, which is not subject to precise definition. To isolate part of life and call it **religion** is to disintegrate life and to distort **religion**. And this is just why the God of worship claims all allegiance or none.

[p. 1121] When certain vacillating and timid mortals attempt to escape from the incessant pressure of evolutionary life, **religion**, as they conceive it, seems to present the nearest refuge, the best avenue of escape. But it is the mission of **religion** to prepare man for bravely, even heroically, facing the vicissitudes of life. **Religion** is evolutionary man's supreme endowment, the one thing which enables him to carry on and "endure as seeing Him who is invisible."

[p. 1116] **Religion** becomes the avenue of man's escape from the material limitations of the temporal and natural world to the supernal realities of the eternal and spiritual world by and through the technique of salvation, the progressive morontia transformation.

[p. 1100] **Religion** is not a specific function of life; rather is it a mode of living. True **religion** is a wholehearted devotion to some reality which the religionist deems to be of supreme value to himself and for all mankind. And the outstanding characteristics of all **religions** are: unquestioning loyalty and wholehearted devotion to supreme values.

[p. 1104] **Religion**,as a human experience, ranges from the primitive fear slavery of the evolving savage up to the sublime and magnificient faith liberty of those civilized mortals who are superbly conscious of sonship with the eternal God.

[p. 1104] **Religion**, the conviction-faith of the personality, can always triumph over the superficially contradictory logic of despair born in the unbelieving material mind. There really is a true and genuine inner voice, that "true light which lights every man who comes into the world." **Religion** *is* faith, trust, and assurance.

[p. 793] **Religion** is the mighty lever that lifts civilization from chaos, but it is powerless apart from the fulcrum of sound and normal mind resting securely on sound and normal heredity.

[p. 1089] True **religion** is a meaningful way of living dynamically face to face with the commonplace realities of everyday life. But if religion is to stimulate

Religion (cont.)

individual development of character and augment integration of personality, it must not be standardized. If it is to stimulate evaluation of experience and serve as a value-lure, it must not be stereotyped. If **religion** is to promote supreme loyalties, it must not be formalized.

[p. 1096] **Religion** is not a technique for attaining a static and blissful peace of mind; it is an impluse for organizing the soul for dynamic service. It is the enlistment of the totality of selfhood in the loyal service of loving God and serving man. **Religion** pays any price essential to the attainment of the supreme goal, the eternal prize.

[p. 1100] But true **religion** is a living love, a life of service. The religionist's detachment from much that is purely temproral and trivial never leads to social isolation, and it should not destroy the sense of humor. Genuine **religion** takes nothing away from human existence, but it does add new meanings to all of life; it generates new types of enthusiasm, zeal, and courage. It may even engender the spirit of the crusader, which is more than dangerous if not controlled by spiritual insight and loyal devotion to the commonplace social obligations of human loyalties.

[p. 1105] **Religion** is, rather, a profoundly deep and actual experience of spiritual communion with the spirit influences resident within the human mind, and as far as such an experience if definable in terms of psychology, it is simply the experience of experiencing the reality of believing in God as the reality of such a purely personal experience.

[p. 1117] **Religion** effectually cures man's sense of idealistic isolation or spiritual loneliness; it enfranchises the believer as a son of God, a citizen at a new and meaningful universe.

[p. 1091] True **religion** is to know God as your Father and man as your brother. **Religion** is not a slavish belief in threats of punishment or magical promises of future mystical regards.

[p. 1093] **Religion** inspires man to live courageously and joyfully on the face of the earth; it joins patience with passion, insight to zeal, sympathy with power, and ideals with energy.

[p. 1107] **Religion** consists not in theologic propositions but in spiritual insight and the sublimity of the souls trust.

[p. 1104] True **religion** is not a system of philosophic belief which can be reasoned out and substantiated by natural proofs, neither is it a fantastic and mystic experience of indescribable feelings of ecstasy which can be enjoyed only by the romantic devotees of mysticism. **Religion** is not the product of reason, but viewed from within, it is altogether reasonable. **Religion** is not derived from the logic of human philosophy, but as a mortal experience it is altogether logical. **Religion** is the experiencing of divinity in the consciousness of a moral being of evolutionary origins it represents true experience with eternal realities in time, the realization of spiritual satisfactions while yet in the flesh.

[p. 1115] True **religion** is that sublime and profound conviction within the soul which compellingly admonishes man that it would be wrong for him not to believe in those morontial realities which consititue his highest ethical and moral concepts, his highest interpretation of life's greatest values and the universe's deepest realities. And such a **religion** is simply the experience of yielding intellectual loyalty to the highest dictates of spiritual consciousness.

[p. 2096] **Religion** is man's supreme experience in the mortal nature but finite language makes it forever impossible for theology ever adequately to depict real religious experience.

[p. 2075] **Religion** is the revelation to man of his divine and eternal destiny.

[p. 2075] **Religion** is designed to find those values in the universe which call forth faith, trust, and assurance; religion culminates in worship. **Religion** discovers for the soul those supreme values which are in contrast with the relative values discovered by the mind. Such superhuman insight can be had only through genuine religious experience.

[p. 1950] This is the essence of true **religion**: that you love your neighbor as yourself.

[p. 1739] **Religion** is the exclusively spiritual experience of the evolving immortal soul of the God-knowing man, but moral power and spiritual energy are mighty forces which may be utilized in dealing with difficult social situations and in solving intricate economic problems. These moral and spiritual endowments make all levels of human living richer and more meaningful.

[p. 1616] True **religion** is the act of an individual soul in its self-conscious relations with the Creator; organized **religion** is man's attempt to socialize the worship of individual religionists.

[p. 1641] **Religion** is a revelation to man's soul dealing with spiritual realities which the mind alone could never fully discover or fully fathom.

[p. 1781] **Religion** reaches out for undiscovered ideals, unexplored realities, superhuman values, divine wisdom, and true spirit attainment. True **religion** does all this; all other beliefs are not worthy of the name.

Resist not evil, *[p. 1590]* And when he said "**Resist not evil,**" he later explained that he did not mean to condone sin or to counsel fraternity with Iniquity. He Intended the more to teach forgiveness, to "**resist not evil** treatment of one's personality, evil injury to one's feelings of personal dignity."

Resurrection of the unjust, *[p. 1247]* The technique of justice demands that personal or group guardians shall respond to the dispensational roll call in behalf of all nonsurviving personalities. The Adjusters of such nonsurvivors do not return, and when the rolls are called, the seraphim respond, but the Adjusters make no answer. This constitutes the "**resurrection of the unjust,**" in reality the formal recognition of the cessation of creature existence. This roll call of justice always immediately follows the roll call of mercy, the resurrection of the sleeping survivors.

Rest, *[p. 299]* **Rest** is of a sevelfold natures; There is the **rest** of sleep and of play in the lower life orders. Discovery in the higher beings, and worship in the highest type of spirit personality. There is also the normal **rest** of energy intake, the recharging of beings with physical or with spiritual energy. And then there is the transit sleep, the unconsicous slumber when enseraphimed, and when in passage from one sphere to another. Entirely different from all of these is the deep sleep of metamorphosis, the transition rest from one stage of being to another, from one life to another, from one state of existence to another, the sleep which ever attands transition from actual universe *status* in contrast to evolution through various *stages* of any one status.

Revelation

Revelation, *[p. 1106]* Reason is the method of science; faith is the method of religion; logic is the attempted technique of philosophy. **Revelation** compensates for the absence of the morontia viewpoint by providing a techinque for achieving unity in the comprehension of the reality and relationships of matter and spirit by the mediation of mind. And true **revelation** never renders science unnatural, religion unreasonable, or philosophy illogical.

[p. 1106] Faith reveals God in the soul. **Revelation**, the substitute for morontia insight on an evolutionary world, enables man to see the same God in nature that faith exhibits in his soul. Thus does **revelation** successfully bridge the gulf between the material and the spiritual, even between the creature and the Creator, between man and God.

[p. 1107] **Revelation** as an epochal phenomenon is periodic; as a personal human experience it is continuous.

[p. 1110] **Revelation** is a techinque whereby ages upon ages of time are saved in the necessary work of sorting and sifting the errors of evolution from the truths of spirit acquirement.

[p. 1122] **Revelation** liberates men and starts them out on the eternal adventure.

Science sorts men; religion loves men, even as yourself; wisdom does justice to differing men; but **revelation** glorifies man and discloses his capacity for partnership with God.

Science vainly strives to create the brotherhood of culture; religion brings into being the brotherhood of the spirit. Philosophy strives for the brotherhood of wisdom; **revelation** portrays the eternal brotherhood, the Paradise Corps of the Finality.

Knowledge yields pride in the fact of personality; widsom is the consciousness of the meaning of personality; religion is the experience of cognizance of the value of personality; **revelation** is the assurance of personality survival. *[p. 1123]* Revealed religion is the unifying element of human existence. **Revelation** unifies history, co-ordinates geology astronomy, physics, chemistry, biology, sociology, and psychology. Spiritual experience is the real soul of man's cosmos.

Revenge, *[p. 1632]* Hate is the shadow of fear; **revenge** the mask of cowardice.

Righteousness, *[p. 238]* Virtue is volitional with personality; **Righteousness** is not automatic in freewill creatures.

Rights, *[p. 794]* When **rights** are old beyond knowledge of origin, they are often called natural **rights**. But human **rights** are not really naturals they are entirely social. They are relative and ever changing, being no more than the rules of the game—recognized adjustments of relations governing the ever-changing phenomena of human competition.

What may be regarded as **right** in one age may not be so regarded in another.

The weak and inferior have always contended for equal **rights**; thay have always insisted that the state compel the strong and superior to supply their wants and otherwise make good those deficiencies which all too often are the natural result of their own indifference and indolence. Society cannot offer equal **rights** to all, but it can promise to administer the varying **rights** of each with fairness and equity.

Ritual, *[p. 992]* The essence of the **ritual** is the perfection of its performance; among savages it must be practiced with exact precision.

Ritual is the technique of sanctifying custom; **ritual** creates and perpetuates myths as well as contributing to the preservation of social and religious customs. Again, **ritual** itself has been fathered by myths. **Rituals** are often at first social, later becoming economic and finally acquiring the sanctity and dignity of religious ceremonial. **Ritual** may be personal or group in practice—or both—as illustrated by prayer, dancing, and drama.

S

Savior, *[p. 2017]* Though it is hardly proper to speak of Jesus as a sacrificer, a ransomer, or a redeemer, it is wholly correct to refer to him as a *savior*. He forever made the way of salvation (survival) more clear and certain; he did better and more surely show the way of salvation for all the mortals of all the worlds of Nebadon.

Science, *[p. 1136]* **Science** is man's attempted study of his physical environment, the world of energy-matter.

[p. 2096] **Science** is man's effort to solve the apparent riddles of the material universe.

Scriptures, *[p. 1767]* These writings are the work of men, some of them holy men, others not so holy. The teachings of these books represent the views and extent of enlightenment of the times in which they had their origin. As a revelation of truth, the last are more dependable than the first. The **Scriptures** are faulty and altogether human in origin, but mistake not, they do constitute the best collection of religious wisdom and spiritual truth to be found in all the world at this time.

Many of these books were not written by the persons whose names they bear, but that in no way detracts from the value of the truths which they contain.

[p. 1768] The **Scriptures** are sacred because they present the thoughts and acts of men who were searching for God, and who in these writings left of record their highest concepts of righteousness, truth, and holiness. The **Scriptures** contain much that is true, very much, but in the light of your present teaching, you know that these writings also contain much that is misrepresentative of the Father in heaven, the loving God I have come to reveal to all the worlds.

[p. 1768] Nathaniel, never permit yourself for one moment to believe the **Scripture** records which tell you that the God of love directed your forefathers to go forth in battle to slay all their enemies—men, woman, and children. Such records are the words of men, not very holy men, and they are not the word of God. The **Scriptures** always have, and always will, reflect the intellectual, moral, and spiritual status of those who create them.

[p. 1768] Nathaniel, never forget, the Father does not limit the revelation of truth to any one generation or to any one people. Many earnest seekers after the truth have been, and will continue to be, confused and disheartened by these doctrines of the perfection of the Scriptures.

Scriptures (cont.)

*[p. 1768]*Mark you well my words, Nathaniel, nothing which human nature has touched can, be regarded as infallible. Through the mind of man divine truth may indeed shine forth, but always of relative purity and partial divinity. The creature may crave infallibility, but only the Creators possess it.

[p. 1768] But the greatest error of the teaching about the **Scriptures** is the doctrine of their being sealed books of mystery and wisdom which only the wise minds of the nation dare to interpret.

[p. 1769] The fear of the authority of the sacred writings of the past effectively prevents the honest souls of today from accepting the new light of the gospel, the light which these very God-knowing men of another generation so intensely longed to see.

Sadducees, *[p. 1534]* The **Sadducees** consisted of the priesthood and certain wealthy Jews. They were not such sticklers for the details of law enforcement. The Pharisees and **Sadducees** were really religious parties, rather than sects.

Salvation, *[p. 1137]* True **salvation** is the technique of the divine evolution of the mortal mind from matter identification through the realms of morontia liaison to the high universe status of spiritual correlation.

[p. 1478] The saving or losing of a soul has to do with whether or not the moral consciousness attains survival status through eternal alliance with its associated immortal spirit endowment. **Salvation** is the spiritualization of the self-realization of the moral consciousness, which thereby becomes possessed of survival value. All forms of soul conflict consist in the lack of harmony between the moral, or spiritual, self-consciousness and the purely intellectual self-consciousness.

[p. 1682] **Salvation** is the gift of the Father and is-revealed by his Sons. Acceptance by faith on your part makes you a partaker of the divine nature, a son or a daughter of God. By faith you are justified; by faith are you saved; and by this same faith are you eternally advanced in the way of progressive and divine perfection.

[p. 1683] You cannot buy **salvation**; you cannot earn righteousness. **Salvation** is the gift of God, and righteousness is the natural fruit of the spirit-born life of sonship in the kingdom. You are not to be saved because you live a righteous life; rather is it that you live a righteous life because you have already been saved, have recognized sonship as the gift of God and service in the kingdom as the supreme delight of life on earth. When men believe this gospel, which is a revelation of the goodness of God, they will be led to voluntary repentance of all known sin. Realization of sonship is incompatible with the desire to sin. Kingdom believers hunger for righteousness and thirst for divine perfection.

[p. 2053] It is your faith that saves your souls. **Salvation** is the gift of God to all who believe they are his sons. But be not deceived; while **salvation** is the free gift of God and is bestowed upon all who accept it by faith, there follows the experience of bearing the fruits of this spirit life as it is lived in the flesh.

[p. 2017] All this concept of atonement and sacrificial **salvation** is rooted and grounded in selfishness. Jesus taught that *service* to one's fellows is the highest concept of the brotherhood of spirit believers. **Salvation** should be taken for granted by those who believe in the fatherhood of God. The believer's chief concern should not be the selfish desire for personal salvation but rather the unselfish urge to love and, therefore, serve one's fellows even as Jesus loved and served mortal men.

Seraphim

Neither do genuine believers trouble themselves so much about the future punishment of sin. The real believer is only concerned about present separation from God. True, wise fathers may chasten their sons, but they do all this in love and for corrective purposes. They do not punish in anger, neither do they chastise in retribution.

Even if God were the stern and legal monarch of a universe in which justice ruled supreme, he certainly would not be satisfied with the childish scheme of substituting an innocent sufferer for a guilty offender.

The great thing about the death of Jesus, as it is related to the enrichment of human experience and the enlargement of the way of **salvation**, is not the *fact* of his death but rather the superb manner and the matchless spirit in which he met death.

This entire idea of the ransom of the atonement places **salvation** upon a plane of unreality; such a concept is purely philosophic. Human **salvation** is *real*; it is based on two realities which may be grasped by the creature's faith and thereby become incorporated into individual human experience; the fact of the fatherhood of God and its correlated truth, the brotherhood of man. It is true, after all, that you are to be "forgiven your debts, even as you forgive your debtors."

Sectarinaism, *[p. 1092]* **Sectarianism** is a disease of institutional religion, and dogmatism is an enslavement of the spiritual nature

Security, *[p. 793]* Society's prime gift to man is **security**.

Segregata, *[p. 126] Pregravity Stages (force).* This is the first step in the individuation of space potency into the pre-energy forms of cosmic force. This state is analogous to the concept of the primordial force-charge of space, sometimes called pure energy, or **segregata**.

[p. 469] Primordial force is sometimes spoken of as pure energy: on Uversa we refer to it as **SEGREGATA**.

Self-Consciousness, *[p. 194]* **Self-consciousness** consists in intellectual awareness of personality actuality; it includes the ability to recognize the reality of other personalities. It indicates capacity for individualized experience in and with cosmic realities, equivalating to the attainment of identity status in the personality relationships of the universe.

Self-control, *[p. 927]* That acme of all human virtues, rugged **self-control**.

Selfishness, *[p. 613]* Unbridled self-will and unregulated self-expression equal unmitigated **selfishness**, the acme of ungodliness

Sensitivity, Ethic. *[p. 646]* Through the realization of truth the appreciation of beauty leads to the sense of the eternal fitness of those things which impinge upon the recognition of divine goodness in Deity relations with all beings; and thus even cosmology leads to the pursuit of divine reality values——to God-consciousness.

Seraphim, *[p. 1241]* These attending **seraphim** have functioned as the spiritual helpers of mortal man in all the great events of the past and the present. In many a revelation "the word was spoken by angels", many of the mandates of heaven have been "received by the ministry of angels." **Seraphim** are the traditional angels of heaven; they are the ministering spirits who live so near you and do so much for you. They have ministered on Urantia since the earliest times of human intelligence.

Service

Service, *[p. 2017]* Jesus taught that **service** to one's fellows is the highest concept of the brotherhood of spirit believers.

Sin, *[p. 754]* There are many ways of looking at **sin**, but from the universe philosophic viewpoint **sin** is the attitude of a personality who is knowlingly reisiting cosmic reality.

[p. 761] **Sin** being an attitude of the person toward reality, is destined to exhibit its inherent negativistic harvest upon any and all related levels of universe values.

[p. 761] **Sin** is fraught with fatal consequences to personality survival only when it is the attitude of the whole being, when it stands for the choosing of the mind and the willing of the soul.

[p. 761] No person is ever made to suffer vital spiritual deprivation because of the **sin** of another. **Sin** is wholly personal as to moral guilt or spiritual consequences, notwithstanding its far-flung repercussions in administrative, intellectual, and social domains.

[p. 984] **Sin** must be redefined as deliberate disloyalty to Deity. There are degrees of disloyalty: the partial loyalty of indecisions the divided loyalty of confliction; the dying loyalty of indifference: and the death of loyalty exhibited in devotion to godless ideals.

The sense or feeling of guilt is the consciousness of the violation of the mores; it is not necessarily **sin**. There is no real **sin** in the absence of conscious disloyalty to Deity.

[p. 1660] **Sin** is the conscious, knowing, and deliberate transgression of the divine law, the Father's will; **Sin** is the measure of unwillingness to be divinely led and spiritually directed.

[p. 1861] Jesus taught that **sin** is not the child of a defective nature but rather the offspring of a knowing mind dominated by an unsubmissive will. Regarding **sin**, he taught that God has forgiven; that we make such forgiveness personally available by the act of forgiving our fellows. When you forgive your brother in the flesh, you thereby create the capacity in your own soul for the reception of the reality of God's forgiveness of your own misdeeds.

[p. 2016] The animal nature——the tendency toward evildoing— may be hereditary, but sin is not transmitted from parent to child. **Sin** is the act of conscious and deliberate rebellion against the Father's will and the Sons' laws by an individual will creature.

Skill, *[p. 1779]* Ability is that which you inherit, while **skill** is what you acquire. Life is not real to one who cannot do some one thing well, expertly. **Skill** is one of the real sources of the satisfaction of living.

Society, *[p. 911]* **Society** is the offspring of age upon age of trial and error; it is what survived the selective adjustments and readjustments in the successive stages of mankind's agelong rise from animal to human levels of planetary status. The great danger to any civilization-at any one moment-is the threat of breakdown during the time of transition from the established methods of the past to those new and better, but untried procedures of the future.

Sonship, *[p. 1621]* In all praying, remember that **sonship** is a *gift*. No child has aught to do with earning the status of son or daughter. The earth child comes into being by the will of its parents. Even so, the child, of God comes into grace and the new life of the spirit by the will of the Father in heaven. Therefore must the Kingdom of heaven——divine **sonship** be received as by a little child. You earn righteousness——progressive character development——but you receive **sonship** by grace and through faith.

Soul, *[p. 8]* The **soul** of man is an experiential acquirement. As a mortal creature chooses to "do the will of the Father in heaven," so the indwelling spirit becomes the father of a new reality in human experience. The mortal and material mind is the mother of this same emerging reality. The substance of this new reality is neither material nor spiritual——it is morontial. This is the emerging and immortal **soul** which is destined to survive mortal death and begin the paradise ascension.

[p. 1218] The human personality is identified with mind and spirit held together in fuctional relationship by life in a material body. This functioning relationship of such mind and spirit does not result in some combination of the qualities or attributes of mind and spirit but rather in an entirely new, original, and unique universe value of potentially eternal endurance, the *soul.*

[p. 1478] The **soul** is the self-reflective, truth-discerning, and spirit-perceiving part of man which forever elevates the human being above the level of the animal world. Self-consciousness, in and of itself, is not the **soul.** Moral self-consciousness is true human self-realization and constitutes the foundation of the human **soul,** and the **soul** is that part of man which represents the potential survival value of human experience. Moral choice and spiritual attainmant, the ability to know God and the urge to be like him, are the characteristics of the **soul.** The **soul** of man cannot exist apart from moral thinking and spiritual activity. A stagnant **soul** is a dying soul. But the **soul** of man is distinct from the divine spirit which dwells within the mind. The divine spirit arrives simultaneously with the first moral activity of the human mind, and that is the occasion of the birth of the **soul.**

[p. 1288] The morontia **soul** of an evolving mortal is really the son of the Adjuster action of the Universal Father and the child of the cosmic reaction of the Supreme Being, the Universal Mother.

Space, *[p. 132]* **Space** is, from the human viewpoint, nothing—— negative; it exists only as related to something positive and nonspatial. **Space** is, however, real. It contains and conditions motion. It even moves.

[p. 1297] Only by ubiquity could Deity unify time-**space** manifestations to the finite conception, for time is a succession of instants while **space** is a system of associated points. You do after all, perceive time by analysis and **space** by synthesis.

[p. 1297] **Space** comes the nearest of all nonabsolute things to being absolute. **Space** is apparently absolutely ultimate. The real difficulty we have in understanding space on the material level is due to the fact that, while material bodies exist in **space, space** also exists in these same material bodies. While there is much about **space** that is absolute, that does not mean that **space** is absolute.

[p. 2021] Mankind is slow to perceive that, in all that is personal, matter is the skeleton of morontia, and that both are the reflected shadow of enduring spirit reality. How long before you will regard time as the moving image of eternity and **space** as the fleeting shadow of Paradise realities?

Space Potency

Space Potency, *[p. 469]* **Space potency** is a prereality; it is the domain of the Unqualified Absolute and is responsive only to the personal grasp of the Universal Father, notwithstanding that it is seemingly modifiable by the presence of the Primary Master Force organizers.

On Uversa, **space potency** is spoken of as ABSOLUTA.

Spirit, *[p. 78]* **Spirit** is ever conscious, minded, and possessed of varied phases of identity. Without mind in some phase there would be no spiritual consciousness in the fraternity of **spirit** beings.

[p. 8] Spirit. The divine **spirit** that indwells the mind of man—the Thought Adjuster. This immortal **spirit** is prepersonal—not a personality, though destined to become a part of the personality of the surviving mortal creature.

[p. 102] Cosmic force responds to mind even as cosmic mind responds to spirit. Spirit is divine purpose, and spirit mind is divine purpose in action. Energy is thing, mind is meaning, **spirit** is value. Even in time and space, mind establishes those relative relationships between energy and **spirit** which are suggestive of mutual kinship in eternity.

[p. 140] The goal of existence of all personalities is **spirit**.

Spirit of God, *[p. 95]* In your sacred writings the term *Spirit of God* seems to be used interchangeably to designate both the infinite Spirit on Paradise and the Creative Spirit of your local universe. The Holy Spirit is the spiritual circuit of this Creative Daughter of the Paradise Infinite Spirit. The Holy Spirit is a circuit indigenous to each local universe and is confined to the spiritual realm of that creation: but the Infinite Spirit is omnipresent.

Spiritual reason, *[p. 1108]* Faith-insight, or spiritual intuition, is the endowment of the cosmic mind in association with the Thought Adjuster, which is the Father's gift to man. **Spiritual reason**, soul intelligence, is the endowment of the Holy Spirit, the Creative Spirit's gift to man. Spiritual philosophy, the wisdom of spirit realities, is the endowment of the Spirit of Truth, the combined gift of the bestowal Sons to the children of men. And the co-ordination and interassociation of these spirit endowments constitute man a spirit personality in potential destiny.

Spirituality, *[p. 1096]* **Spirituality** becomes at once the indicator of one's nearness to God and the measure of one's usefulness to fellow beings. **Spirituality** enhances the ability to discover beauty in things, recognize truth in meanings, and discover goodness in values. Spiritual development is determined by capacity therefor and is directly proportional to the elimination of the selfish qualities of love.

Spironga, *[p. 416]* The **Spironga** are the spirit offspring of the Bright and Morning Star and the Father Melchizedek. They are exempt from personality termination but are not evolutionary or ascending beings. Niether are they functionally concerned with the evolutionary ascension regime. They are the spirit helpers of the local universe, executing the routine spirit tasks of Nebadon.

Spornagia, *[p. 416]* The architectural headquarters worlds of the local universe are real worlds—physical creations. There is much work connected with their physical upkeep, and herein we have the assistance of a group of physical creatures called **spornagia**. They are devoted to the care and culture of the material phases of these headquarters worlds, from Jerusem to Salvington. **Spornagia** are neither spirits not persons; they are an animal order of existence, but if you could see them, you would agree that they seem to be perfect animals.

[p. 528] **Spornagia** are not Adjuster indwelt. They do not possess survival souls, but they do enjoy long lives, sometimes to the extent of forty to fifty thousand standard years. Their number is legion, and they afford physical ministry to all orders of universe personalities requiring material service.

Although **spornagia** neither possess nor evolve survival souls, though they do not have personality, nevertheless, they do evolve an individuality which can experience reincarnation. When, with the passing of time, the physical bodies of these unique creatures deteriorate from usage and age, their creators in collaboration with the Life Carters, fabricate new bodies in which the old **spornagia** re-establish their residences.

Spornagia are the only creatures in all the universe of Nebadon who experience this or any other sort of reincarnation.

[p. 523] Perhaps I can best suggest to Urantia minds something of the nature of these beautiful and serviceable creatures by saying that they embrace the combined traits of a faithful horse and an affectionate dog and manifest an intelligence exceeding that of the highest type of chimpanzee.

Subabsolute Inevitability, *[p. 185]* We have come to speak of the threefold personalization of Deity as the absolute inevitability, while we have come to look upon the appearance of the Seven Master Spirits as the **subabsolute inevitability**.

Subpersonal, *[p. 78]* Man also observes mind phenomena in living organisms functioning on the **subpersonal** (animal) level.

Superuniverse, *[p. 166]* Ten major sectors (about 1,000,000,000 inhabited worlds) make one major sector. Each major sector is provided with an enormous and glorous headquarters world and is ruled by three Ancients of Days.

Supreme Being, *[p. 11]* The **Supreme Being** is not a direct creator, except that he Is the father of Majeston, but he is a synthetic co-ordinator of all creature-Creator universe activities. The **Supreme Being**, now actualizing in the evolutionary universes, is the Deity correlator and synthesizer of time-space divinity, of triune Paradise Deity in experiential association with the Supreme Creators of time and space.

Survival, *[p. 404]* The **survival** of mortal creatures is wholly predicated on the evolvement of an immortal soul within the mortal mind.

[p. 761] Eternal **survival** can be jeopardized only by the decisions of the mind and the choice of the soul of the individual himself.

[p. 2095] Human **survival** is in great measure dependent on consecrating the human will to the choosing of those values selected by this spirit-value sorter— the indwelling interpreter and unifier.

Suspicion, *[p. 437]* **Suspicion** is the inherent reaction of primitive men; the survival struggles of the early ages do not naturally breed trust.

System, *[p. 166]* The basic unit of the supergovernment consists of about one thousand inhabited or inhabitable worlds. Blazing suns, cold worlds, planets too near the hot suns, and other spheres not suitable for creature habitation are not included in this group. These one thousand worlds adapted to support life are called

Tact

a **system**, but in the younger **systems** only a comparatively small number of these worlds may be inhabited. Each inhabited planet is presided over by a Planetary Prince, and each local **system** has an architectural sphere as its headquarters and is ruled by a **System** Sovereign.

T

Tact, *[p. 1740]* As you grow older in years and more experienced in the affairs of the kingdom, are you becoming more **tactful** in dealing with troublesome mortals and more tolerant in living with stubborn associates? **Tact** is the fulcrum of social leverage, and tolerance is the earmark of a great soul. If you possess these rare and charming gifts, as the days pass you will become more alert and expert in your worthy efforts to avoid all unnecessary social misunderstandings. Such wise souls are able to avoid much of the trouble which is certain to be the portion of all who suffer from lack of emotional adjustment, those who refuse to grow up, and those who refuse to grow old gracefully.

Theology, *[p. 1130]* That religionists have believed so much that was false does not invalidate religion because religion is founded on the recognition of values and is validated by the faith of personal religious experience. Religion, then, is based on experience and religious thought; **theology**, the philosophy of religion, is an honest attempt to interpret that experience. Such interpretative beliefs may be right or wrong, or a mixture of truth and error.

[p. 1135] **Theology** is the study of the actions and reactions of the human spirit; it can never become a science since it must always be combined more or less with psychology in its personal expression and with philosophy in its systematic portrayal. **Theology** is always the study of *your* religion; the study of another's religion is psychology.

Thor, *[p. 893]* The decisive struggles between the white man and the blue man were fought out in the valley of the Somme. Here the flower of the blue race bitterly contested the southward moving Andites, and for over five hundred years these Cro-Magnoids successfully defended their territories before succumbing to the superior military strategy of the white invaders. **Thor**, the victorious commander of the armies of the north in the final battle of the Somme, became the hero of the northern tribes and later on was revered as a god by some of them.

Thought Adjuster, *[p. 1129]* The **Thought Adjuster** is the cosmic window through which the finite creature may faith-glimpse the certainties and divinities of limitless Deity, the Universal Father.

[p. 1176] It is the **Adjuster** who creates within man that unquenchable yearning and incessant longing to be like God, to attain Paradise, and there before the actual person of Deity to worship the infinite source of the divine gift. The **Adjuster** is the living presence which actually links the mortal son with his Paradise Father and draws him nearer and nearer to the father. The **Adjuster** is our compensatory equalization of the enormous universe tension which is created by the distance of man's removal from God and by the degree of his partiality in contrast with the universality of the eternal Father.

Thought Adjuster

The **Adjuster** is an absolute essence of an infinite being imprisioned within the mind of a finite creature which, depending on the choosing of such a mortal, can eventually consummate this temporary union of God and man and veritably actualize a new order of being for unending universe service. The **Adjuster** is the divine universe reality which factualizes the truth that God is man's Father. The **Adjuster** is man's infallible cosmic compass, always and unerringly pointing the soul Godward.

[p. 1176] The **Adjusters** are the actuality of the Father's love incarnate in the souls of men; they are the veritable promise of man's eternal career imprisoned within the mortal mind; they are the essence of man's perfected finaliter personality, which he can foretast in time as he progressively masters the divine technique of achieving the living of the Father's will, step by step, through the ascension of universe upon universe until he actually attains the divine presence of his Paradise Father.

[p. 1177] Together with their many unrevealed associates, the **Adjusters** are undiluted and unmixed divinity, unqualified and unattenuated parts of Deity; they are of God, and as far as we are able to discern, **they are God**.

[p. 1182] The **Adjuster** is man's eternity possibility, man is the **Adjusters** personality possibility.

[p. 1183] **Thought Adjusters** are not personalities, but they are real entities; they are truly and perfectly individualized, although they are never, while indwelling mortals, actually personalized. **Thought Adjusters** are not true personalities; the are *true realities*, realities of the purest order known in the universe of universes—they are the divine presence.

[p. 1193] The **Adjuster** is the wellspring of spiritual attainment and the hope of divine character within you. He is the power, privilege, and the possibility of survival, which so fully and forever distinguishes you from mere animal creatures, he is the higher and truly interanl spiritual stimulus of thought in contrast with the external and physical stimulus, which reaches the mind over the nerve-energy mechanism of the material body.

These faithful custodians of the future career unfailingly duplicate every mental creation with a spiritual counterpart: they are thus slowly and surely re-creating you as you really are (only spiritually) for resurrection on the survival worlds. And all of these exquisite spirit re-creations are being preserved; in the emerging reality of your evolving and immortal soul, your morontia self. These realities are actually there, notwithstanding that the **Adjuster** is seldom able to exalt these duplicate creations sufficiently to exhibit then to the light of consciousness.

And as you are the human parent, so is the **Adjuster** the divine parent of the real you, your higher and advancing self, your better morontial and future spiritual self. And it is this evolving morontial soul that the judges and censors discern when they decree your survival and pass you upward to new worlds, and never ending existence in eternal liaison with your faithful partner—God, the **Adjuster**.

The Adjusters are the eternal ancestors, the divine originals, of your evolving immortal souls; they are the unceasing urge that leads man to attempt the mastery of the material and present existence in the light of the spiritual and future career. The Moni-

Thought Adjusters (cont.)

tors are the prisoners of undying hope, the founts of everlasting progression. And how they do enjoy communicating with their subjects in more or less direct channels! How they rejoice when they can dispense with symbols and other methods of indirection and flash their messages straight to the intellects of their human partners!

[p. 1216] Material evolution has provided you a life machine, your body; the Father himself has endowed you with the purest spirit reality known in the universe, your **Thought Adjuster**. But into your hands, subject to your own decision's, has been given mind, and it is by mind that you live or die. It is within this mind and with this mind that you make those moral decisions which enable you to Achieve Adjusterlikeness, and that is Godlikeness.

[p. 1217] Mind is your ship, the **Adjuster** is your pilot, the human will is captain. The master of the mortal vessel should have the wisdom to trust the divine pilot to guide the ascending soul into the morontia harbors of eternal survival.

Time, *[p. 1297]* Only by ubiquity could Deity unify **time**-space manifestations to the finite conception, for time is a succession of instants while space is a system of associated points. You do, after all, perceive **time** by analysis and space by synthesis.

[p. 1439] **Time** is the stream of flowing temporal events perceived by creature consciousness. **Time** is a name given to the succession arrangement whereby events are recognized and segregated. The universe of space is a **time**-related phenomenon as it is viewed from any interior position outside of the fixed abode of Paradise. The motion of **time** is only revealed in relation to something which does not move in space as a time phenomenon. In the universe of universes Paradise and its Deities transcend both time and space. In the inhabited worlds, human personality (indwelt and oriented by the Paradise Father's spirit) is the only physically related reality which can transcend the material sequence of temporal events.

Animals do not sense **time** as does man, and even to man, beacuse of his sectional and circumscribed view, **time** appears as a succession of events; but as man ascends, as he progresses inward, the enlarging view of this event procession is such that it is discerned more and more in its wholeness. That which formerly appeared as a succession of events then will be viewed as a whole and perfectly related cycle; in this way will circular simultaneity increasingly displace the one-**time** consciousness of the linear sequence of events.

[p. 2021] Mankind is slow to perceive that, in all that is personal, matter is the skeleton of morontia, and that both are the reflected shadow of enduring spirit reality. How long before you will regard **time** as the moving image of eternity and space as the fleeting shadow of Paradise realities?

Totemism, *[p. 970]* **Totemism** is a combination of social and religious observances. Originally it was thought that respect for the totem animal of supposed biologic origin insured the food supply. Totems were at one and the same time symbols of the group and their god. Such a god was the clan personified. **Totemism** was one phase of the attempted socialization of otherwise personal religion. The totem eventually evolved into the flag, or national symbol, of the various modern peoples.

Tranosta, *[p. 471]* Transcendental energy. This energy system operates on and from the upper level of Paradise and only in connection with the absonite peoples. On Uversa it is denominated **TRANOSTA**.

Trinity, Absolute, *[p. 16] The **Absolute Trinity**——the second experiential Trinity——now in process of actualization, will consist of God the Supreme, God the Ultimate, and the unrevealed Consummator of Universe Destiny. This Trinity functions on both personal and superpersonal levels, even to the borders of the nonpersonal, and its unification in universality would experientialize Absolute Deity.

Trinity, Paradise, *[p. 15] The **Paradise Trinity**——the eternal Deity union of the Universal Father, the Eternal Son, and the Infinite Spirit——is existential in actuality, but all potentials are experiential. Therefore does this Trinity constitute the only Deity reality embracing infinity, and therefore do there occur the universe phenomena of the actualization of God the Supreme, God the Ultimate, and God the Absolute.

Trinity, Ultimate, *[p. 16] The **Ultimate Trinity**, now evolving, will eventually consist of the Supreme Being, the Supreme Creator Personalities, and the absonite Architects of the Master Universe, those unique universe planners who are neither creators not creatures. God the Ultimate will eventually and enevitably powerize and personalize as the Deity consequence of the unification of this experiential Ultimate Trinity in the expanding arena of the well-nigh limitless master universe.

Truth, *[p. 42] Physical facts are fairly uniform, but **truth** is a living and flexible factor in the philosophy of the universe.

*[p. 42] **Truth** is beautiful because it is both replete and symmetrical. When man searches for **truth**, he pursues the divinely real.

*[p. 42] Divine **truth** is best known by its *spiritual flavor*.

*[p. 647] **Truth** is the basis of science and philosophy, presenting the intellectual foundation of religion.

*[p. 883] However wise it may be to glean wisdom from the past, it is folly to regard the past as the exclusive source of **truth**. **Truth** is relative and expanding; it *lives* always in the present, acheiving new expression in each generation of men—even in each human life.

[p. 1138] The **truth**——an understanding of cosmic relationships, universe facts, and spiritual values——can best be had through the ministry of the Spirit of **Truth** and can best be criticized by *revelation*. But revelation originates neither a science nor a religion; its function is to co-ordinate both science and religion with the **truth** of reality.

[p. 1297] Things are time conditioned, but **truth** is timeless. The more **truth** you know, the more **truth** you *are*, the more of the past you can understand and of the future you can comprehend.

Truth is inconcussible——forever exempt from all transient vicissitudes, albeit never dead and formal, always vibrant and adaptable——radiantly alive. But when **truth** becomes linked with fact, then both time and space condition its meanings and correlate its values. Such realities of truth wedded to fact become concepts and are accordingly relegated to the domain of relative cosmic realities.

[p. 1459] Truth cannot be Defined with words, only by living. Truth is always more than knowledge. Knowledge pertains to things observed, but truth transcends such purely material levels in that it consorts with wisdom and embraces

such imponderables as human experience even spiritual and living realities. Knowledge originates in science; wisdom, in true philosophy; truth, in the religious experience of spiritual living. Knowledge deals with facts; wisdom with relationships: truth, with reality values.

[p. 1459] Revealed **truth**, personally discovered **truth**, is the supreme delight of the human soul.

[p. 1949] Divine **truth** is a spirit-discerned and living reality. **Truth** exists only on high spiritual levels of the realization of divinity and the consciousness of communion with God. You can know the **truth**, and you can live the **truth**; you can experience the growth of **truth** in the soul and enjoy the liberty of its enlightenment in the mind, but you cannot imprison truth in formulas, codes, creeds, or intellectual patterns of human conduct. When you undertake the human formulation of divine **truth**, it speedily dies.

[p. 2075] **Truth** often becomes confusing and even misleading when it is dismembered, segregated, isolated, and too much analyzed. Living **truth** teaches the **truth** seeker aright only when it is embraced in wholeness and as a living spiritual reality, not as a fact of material science or an inspiration of intervening art.

U

Ultimata, [p. 126] *Gravity Stages (Energy).* This modification of the force charge of space is produced by the action of the Paradise force organizers. It signalizes the appearance of energy systems responsive to the null of paradise gravity. This emergent energy is originally neutral but consequent upon further metamorphosis will exhibit the so-called negative and positive qualities. We designate these stages *Ultimata*.

[p. 470] Puissant and gravity energies, when regarded collectively are spoken of an Uversa as *ULTIMATA*.

Understanding, [p. 402] The impulse of co-ordination, the spontaneous and apparently automatic association of ideas. This is the gift of the co-ordination of acquired knowledge, the phenomenon of quick reasoning, rapid judgement, and prompt decision.

[p. 1219] Recognition is the intellectual process of fitting the sensory impressions received from the external world into the memory patterns of the individual. **Understanding** connotes that these recognized sensory impressions and their associated memory patterns have become integrated or organized into a dynamic network of principles.

Unions of Days, [p. 179] The Paradise advisers to the rulers of the local universes.

Universal Father, [p. 5] God——the **Universal Father**—— is the personality of the First Source and Center and as such maintains personal realtions of Infinite control over all co-ordinate and subordinate sources and centers.

[p. 8] The **Universal Father** is the secret of the reality of personality, the bestowal of personality, and the destiny of personality.

[p. 21] The **Universal Father** is the God of all creation, the First Source and

Center of all things and beings. First think of God as a creator, then as a controller, and lastly as an infinite upholder.

[p. 34] The **Universal Father** is absolutely and without qualification infinite in all his attributes; and this fact, in and of itself, automatically shuts him off from all direct personal communication with finite material beings and other lowly created intelligences.

[p. 74] The **Universal Father** never personally functions as a creator except in conjunction with the Son or with the co-ordinate action of the Son.

Universe of Universes, [p. 637] The **universe of universes** is one vast integrated mechanism which is absolutely controlled by one infinite mind.

Univitatia, [p. 493] **Univitatia** are the permanent citizens of Edentia and its associated worlds, all seven hundred seventy worlds surrounding the constellation headquarters being under their supervision. These children of the Creator Son and the Creative Spirit are projected on a plane of existence in between the material and the spiritual, but they are not morontia creatures.

Unpervaded space, [p. 123] **"Unpervaded"** space means: unpervaded by those forces, energies, powers, and presences known to exist in pervaded space.

Unselfishness, [p. 51] The spirit of self-forgetfulness.

Urantia, [p. 1] **Urantia**——that being the name of your world.

Utopia, evolutionary, [p. 567] This epoch of the Teacher Sons is the vestibule to the final planetary age——**evolutionary utopia**——the age of light and life.

V

Vanity, [p. 776] The longing to display one's property accumulations.

Violence, [p. 783] **Violence** is the law of nature, hostility the automatic reaction of the children of nature, while war is but these same activities carried on collectively.

Virtue, [p. 193] **Virtue** is righteousness——conformity with the cosmos. To name **virtues** is not to define them, but to live them is to know them. **Virtue** is not mere knowledge nor yet wisdom but rather the reality of progressive experience in the attainment of ascending levels of cosmic achievement. In the day by day life of mortal man, **virtue** is realized by the consistent choosing of good rather then evil, and such choosing ability is evidence of the possession of a moral nature.

[p. 193] Supreme **virtue**, then, is wholeheartedly to choose to do the will of the Father in heaven.

[p. 238] **Virtue** is volitional with personality; righteousness is not automatic in freewill creatures.

W

War, [p. 783] **War** is the natural state and heritage of evolving man; peace is the social yardstick measuring civilization's advancement.

[p. 783] **War** is an animalistic reaction to misunderstandings and irritations; peace attends upon the civilized solution of all such problems and difficulties.

War (cont.)

[p. 785] In past ages a fierce **war** would institute social changes and facilitate the adoption of new ideas such as would not have occurred naturally in ten thousand years. The terrible price paid for these certain **war** advantages was that society was temporarily thrown back into savagery; civilized reason had to abdicate, war is strong medicine, very costly and most dangerous; while often curative of certain social disorders, it sometimes kills the patient, destroys the society.

[p. 785] **War** has had a certain evolutionary and selective value, but like slavery, it must sometime be abandoned as civilization slowly advances.

[p. 786] Ancient warfare resulted in the decimation of inferior peoples; the net result of modern conflict is the selective destruction of the best human stocks.

[p. 786] Do not make the mistake of glorifying **war**.

Will, *[p. 730]* Human **will**—the ability to know God and the power of choosing to worship him.

[p. 1431] The **will** of God is the way of God, partnership with the choice of God in the face of any potential alternative. The **will** of man is the way of man, the sum and substance of that which the mortal chooses to be and do. **Will** is the deliberate choice of a self-conscious being which leads to decision-conduct based on intelligent reflection.

[p. 1431] **Will** is that manifestation of the human mind which enables the subjective consciousness to express itself objectively. and to experience the phenomenon of aspiring to be Godlike.

Wisdom, *[p. 216]* **Wisdom** Is twofold in origin, being derived from the perfection of divine insight inherent in perfect beings and from the personal experience acquired by evoltuionary creatures.

[p. 402] The inherent tendency of all moral creatures towards orderly and progressive evolutionary advancement.

[p. 614] Even **wisdom** is divine and safe only when it is cosmic in scope and spiritual in motivation.

[p. 908] Knowledge can be had by education, but **wisdom**, which is indispensable to true culture, can be secured only through experience and by men and women who are innately intelligent. Such a people are able to learn from experience; they may become truly wise.

[p. 1122] Knowledge leads to placing men, to originating social strata and castes; Religion leads to serving men, thus creating ethics and altruism. **Wisdom** leads to the higher and better fellowship of both ideas and one's fellows. Revelation liberates men and starts them out on the eternal adventure.

[p. 1780] The career of a God-seeking man may prove to be a great success in the light of eternity, even though the whole temporal-life enterprise may appear as an overwhelming failure, provided each life failure yielded the culture of **wisdom** and spirit achievement. Do not make the mistake of confusing knowledge, culture, and **wisdom**. They are related in life, but they represent vastly differing spirit values; **widsom** ever dominates knowledge and always glorifies culture.

Work, *[p. 435]* It is not so much what you learn in this first life; it is the experience of living this life that is important. Even the *work* of this world, paramount though it is, is not nearly so important as the *way* in which you do this **work**.

Worship

World, *[p. 1675]* Jesus hardly regarded this **world** as a "vale of tears." He rather looked upon it as the birth sphere of the eternal and immortal spirits of paradise ascension, the "vale of soul making".

Worship, *[p. 192] Worship*—the spiritual domain of the reality of religious experience, the personal realization of divine fellowship, the recognition of spirit values, the assurance of eternal survival, the ascent from the status of servants of God to the joy and liberty of the sons of God. This is the highest insight of the cosmic mind, the reverential and worshipful form of the cosmic discrimination.

[p. 303] **Worship** is the highest privilege and the first duty of all created intelligences. **Worship** is the conscious and joyous act of recognizing and acknowledging the truth and fact of the intimate and personal relationships of the Creators with their creatures. The quality of **worship** is determined by the depth of creature perception; and as the knowledge of the infinite character of the Gods progresses, the act of **worship** becomes increasingly all-encompassing until it eventually attains the glory of the highest experiential delight and the most exquisite pleasure known to created beings.

[p. 304] **Worship** is the highest joy of Paradise existence; it is the refreshing play of Paradise. What play does for your jaded minds on earth, **worship** will do for your perfected souls on Paradise. The mode of **worship** on Paradise is utterly beyond mortal comprehension, but the spirit of it you can begin to appreciate even down here on Urantia, for the spirits of the Gods even now indwell you, hover over you, and inspire you to true **worship**.

[p. 195] **Worship**, the sincere pursuit of divine values and the wholehearted love of the divine Value-Giver.

[p. 402] **Worship** is the badge of spiritual-ascension candidacy.

[p. 1616] **Worship**—contemplation of the spiritual—must alternate with service, contact with material reality.

*[p. 1616]***Worship** is Intended to anticipate the better life ahead and, then to reflect these new spiritual significances back onto the life which now is. Prayer is spiritually sustaining, but **worship** is divinely creative.

Worship is the technique of looking to the *One* for the inspiration of service to the *many*. **Worship** is the yardstick which measures the extent of the soul's detachment from the material universe and its simultaneous and secure attachment to the spiritual realities of all creation.

Prayer is self-reminding—sublime thinking; **worship** is self-forgetting—superthinking. **Worship** is effortless attention, true and ideal soul rest, a form of restful spiritual exertion.

Worship is the act of a part identifying itself with the whole; the finite with the infinite; the son with the Father; time in the act of striking step with eternity. **Worship** is the act of the son's personal communion with the divine Father, the assumption of refreshing, creative, fraternal, and romantic attitudes by the human soul-spirit.

*[p. 2095]*True religious **worship** is not a futile monologue of self-deception. **Worship** is a personal communion with that which is divinely real, with that which is the very source of reality. Man aspires by **worship** to be better and thereby eventually attains the *best*.

Y

Yahweh, *[p. 1053]* **Yahweh** was the god of the southern Palestinian tribes, who associated this concept of deity with Mount Horeb, the Sinai volcano. **Yahweh** was merely one of the hundreds and thousands of nature gods which held the attention and claimed the worship of the Semitic tribes and peoples.

Year, Jerusem, *[p. 519]* The Satania day equals three days of Urantia time, less one hour, four minutes, and fifteen seconds, that being the time of the axial revolution of Jerusem. The system year consists of one hundred Jerusem days.

Year, Nebadon, *[p. 372]* The **Nebadon year** consists of a segment of time of universe swing in relation to the Uversa circuit and is equal to one hundred days of standard universe time, about five years of Urantia time.

KEYWORD INDEX

To the Table of Contents of
The Urantia Book

HOW TO USE THE KEYWORD INDEX:

There are two tables of contents in *The Urantia Book*. This Keyword Index is taken entirely from the second one, entitled "Contents of the Book" and found on pages xii through lxvi. It is a noninterpretive, alphabetical sorting of the significant words of each listing in that section.

The first entry under Z is "Zaccheus, The Visit to, 1873." This tells you that the section entitled "The Visit to Zaccheus" is found on page 1873.

Listings in full capitals denote a paper title. Please note that the alphabetization convention used in this index sorts apostrophes, commas, and hyphens after letters. For example:

> Adjuster to time, Insensitivity of
>
> Adjuster's mission, The
>
> Adjuster, Co-operation with the
>
> Adjuster-fusion series
>
> Adjusters after Death.

We hope that this Keyword Index helps you in your study of the teachings of *The Urantia Book*.

C

D

E

H

N

S

U

www.ingramcontent.com/pod-product-compliance
Ingram Content Group UK Ltd.
Pitfield, Milton Keynes, MK11 3LW, UK
UKHW041323190726
13851UKWH00013B/80

9 780942 430936